"From the leading Australian scholars in the field, this ᴅᴏᴏᴋ ꜱᴇɪ ᴠᴇꜱ as a well-informed call-to-action for achieving a new social contract that addresses the close connections across work, family and caregiving responsibilities. It is a must-read for policymakers."
— *Thomas A. Kochan, Emeritus Professor, MIT Sloan School of Management*

"The ideal policy book: documenting current arrangements, distilling the debates shaping public discussion and directing our thoughts to avenues for change that will make Australia a better place for all."
— *Gabrielle Meagher, Professor Emerita, Macquarie School of Social Sciences*

"This important book provides invaluable guidance for this urgent task, offering deep insights into the whys and hows of new policy directions needed in Australia."
— *Peter Moss, Emeritus Professor, Institute of Education, University College London*

"As the editors of this inspiring collection say, work, care and family policy are at a turning point in Australia as elsewhere. Their collection provides an excellent opportunity for us all to learn from the different policies that have been pursued there, and persuasively sets out possible pathways towards a new and more equitable future. It provides readers with an accessible and comprehensive account of how Australia has arrived at its current turning point and the potential benefits to us all of changing the way work and care are organised."
— *Susan Himmelweit, Emeritus Professor of Economics, The Open University*

"Structured around the life course, *At a Turning Point* makes work, care and family academic and policy debates readily accessible and provides a policy framework for developing gender-equalising policy development."
— *Alexandra Heron, PhD*

At a Turning Point

Work, care and family policies in

Australia

PUBLIC AND SOCIAL POLICY SERIES

Gaby Ramia, Series Editor

The Public and Social Policy series publishes books that pose challenging questions about policy from national, comparative and international perspectives. The series explores policy design, implementation and evaluation; the politics of policy making; and analyses of particular areas of public and social policy.

At a Turning Point

Work, care and family policies in
Australia

Edited by Marian Baird, Elizabeth Hill
and Sydney Colussi

SYDNEY UNIVERSITY PRESS

First published by Sydney University Press
© Individual authors 2024
© Sydney University Press 2024

Sydney University Press
Gadigal Country
Fisher Library F03
University of Sydney NSW 2006
Australia
sup.info@sydney.edu.au
sydneyuniversitypress.com.au

A catalogue record for this book is available from the National Library of Australia.

ISBN 9781743328965 paperback
ISBN 9781743328989 epub
ISBN 9781743328972 pdf

Cover design by Nathan Grice
Cover image: Frogella.stock/Adobe Stock

We acknowledge the traditional owners of the lands on which Sydney University Press is located, the Gadigal people of the Eora Nation, and we pay our respects to the knowledge embedded forever within the Aboriginal Custodianship of Country.

Contents

Abbreviations

ART	assisted reproductive technologies
CCS	Commonwealth Child Care Subsidy scheme
CHSP	Commonwealth Home Support Programme
COTANSW	Council on the Ageing NSW
DaPP	Dad and Partner Pay
ECEC	Early Childhood Education and Care
EMTR	effective marginal tax rate
FCA	Federal Court of Australia
FDC	Family Day Care
FTB A	Family Tax Benefit A
FTB B	Family Tax Benefit B
GEWL	Gender Equality in Working Life
HCPP	Home Care Packages Program
IFA	individual flexibility arrangements
LDC	Long Day Care
NDIA	National Disability Insurance Agency
NDIS	National Disability Insurance Scheme
OSHC	Outside School Hours Care
PLP	Parental Leave Pay
PPL	Paid Parental Leave
WDR	workforce disincentive rate

Preface

The phrases "work and family" and "work and care" are on everyone's lips these days, but it is hard to believe that it is only since 2010 that Australia has had a paid parental leave scheme and a right to request flexible work – a long time after many other countries implemented such measures. These policies are now embedded in our policy framework, but new challenges continue to arise, especially around policy solutions to early childhood education and care, elder care, ageing workforces and fertility. A network of partial and disconnected public policies has developed in response to these problems of contemporary Australia, but understanding and navigating these policies is difficult.

It was in this context and for a number of reasons that we were motivated to produce this book. First and foremost, the need to record, chart and critique the development of work, care and family policies in Australia. Second, the need to offer progressive ideas for the development of more gender-equitable and sustainable policies that reflect the changing profile of Australians, their families and communities. Third, the need to provide to the public, students and policymakers an accessible account and explanation of the complexity of Australia's work, care and family policy architecture.

Since Federation in 1901, the development of Australia's welfare and industrial relations systems has laid the foundation for the wide variety of policies that makes up our work, care and family infrastructure, which in many ways is different to that found in other countries. This institutional history partially explains the complexity of our systems, but so too does the history of the very different political ideologies which have imbued our policy framework. From welfare and social services derived from a government-funded and -controlled system to social services closely tied to employment and privatised delivery, the changes in work and care policy over recent decades have been dramatic. However, we know they are not perfect and not operating to benefit all Australians.

When we started this project, work, care and family policies in Australia were at absolute breaking point and there was increasing frustration with the policy context. Australian women and families were suffering from constant pressure and tension. This was manifested in declining fertility rates, increased stress at work and in the home, and an ongoing unequal sharing of care between women and men. We are now in a different policy environment, but there is still much to be done, and new issues and challenges constantly arise. The task, we felt, was to document the "turning point" we are now at and to ensure we make the most of the new direction and opportunities.

Who better to provide the history and examination of our system than a group of dedicated work, care and family scholars with whom we have worked for many years? They bring years of experience and a variety of disciplinary backgrounds – sociology, political economy, industrial relations, health, policy and law. In September 2018 many of us were together in Melbourne, at the annual Australian Work and Family Policy Roundtable meeting, reporting on changes to the various work, care and family policies and the many areas needing more attention. The COVID-19 pandemic intervened just over a year later and brought to a head the gaps and problems in Australia's work, care and family policy system. The Melbourne meeting demonstrated the depth of expertise and commitment of our colleagues and it struck us as knowledge that needed to be captured and disseminated to a wider audience. It is this wealth of knowledge that we share with you in this book. As we finalise the manuscript, the debate about work and family and work and care remains ongoing with multiple policy innovations under review. We hope you gain new insights from this book and with them feel empowered to contribute to the policy debates and argue for change that delivers better work and better care for all.

Marian Baird, Elizabeth Hill and Sydney Colussi

1
The Australian policy context: Opportunities for a new social and gender contract

Elizabeth Hill and Marian Baird

1.1 Introduction

It is time to remake our society, workplaces and care infrastructures. Weary and whiplashed from the cross-currents of almost three years of pandemic life followed by a cost of living crisis, Australian families and communities are struggling to manage their work, care and family responsibilities, with devastating consequences for wellbeing and economic security (International Labour Organization 2021; OECD 2021; Work + Family Policy Roundtable 2020). Mismatch between the demands of work and the need to care for family is not a new problem, but the pandemic exposed in full glare the fractures, tensions and contradictions embedded in our current work and care arrangements.

The daily juggle millions of Australians face trying to balance their paid work and unpaid care responsibilities is widely reported and debated. The need for change was recognised by the electorate at the May 2022 federal election when Labor won office with reforms to child care and aged care central to its pitch to voters. The government's Jobs and Skills Summit held in Canberra a few months later then catapulted gender equality and the policies needed to achieve this goal to the forefront of public policy.

We are now *at a turning point* in work, care and family policy. This book documents how and why a decade of lost opportunity combined with the pressures of COVID-19 saw work and care policy in Australia reach breaking point. We argue that to meet the economic, social and environmental challenges of the 21st century, a new social contract is required – one that explicitly acknowledges gender and takes a life course approach to work and care policy settings. The pressing need of the current time is a gender and social contract that justly recognises the paid work women do and guarantees everyone a right to care, and to be cared for, over the life course (Work + Family Policy Roundtable 2020, 2022). In this book, we argue a new social contract that better recognises the role of women and supports the interconnections of work and care across society and the economy will deliver significant benefits for families, community and the economy.

1.2 Timing: The urgent need to turn policy around

The pandemic disruption to work, the lockdowns, and work-from-home orders produced an intensification of care and domestic labour that was disproportionately borne by women – especially mothers (Craig & Churchill 2021; Macdonald et al. 2020). For decades, research has shown that unpaid domestic and care labour is not shared equally (Chapman et al. 2014; Pocock et al. 2012; Pocock 2003). Women in Australia and across the world shoulder most of the cleaning, food preparation and family care – even as they continue their steady rise into paid employment (Charmes 2019; UN Women 2018; Craig & Sawrikar 2009). During the pandemic, women added supervising remote school learning of children to their list of daily tasks (Patty & Wade 2021; Macdonald et al. 2020). Initially, men did step up and take on a portion of the extra pandemic unpaid care load (Craig & Churchill 2021), which led to some experts foreshadowing a fundamental shift in the gender division of labour (Alon et al. 2020). However, neither Australian nor global data post-COVID show any realignment in men and women's relative contribution to paid and unpaid labour (UN Women 2020) and very few countries implemented COVID-19 policies to address unpaid labour (UN Women and UNDP 2022).

At the same time, the Australian Commonwealth and some state and territory governments, like many others around the world, have an official commitment to increasing women's labour force participation (New South Wales Government 2022; Australian Government 2017). The Women's Budget Statement 2022–23 notes that advancing gender equality in paid work is a national priority "critical to Australia's economic prosperity and resilience" (Australian Government 2022: 1). But who will take on the care work at home and in the community once women enter the paid workforce? The need for investment in new policy settings to support women's economic opportunities and productivity, such as early childhood education and care, paid parental leave, and respect at work, was one of the key messages to come out of the national Jobs and Skills Summit in September 2022.

Young Australian women are among the most educated in the OECD, with more than half of those aged between 25 and 34 holding a university degree, compared with only one in three men (Australian Bureau of Statistics 2022). High levels of education translate into strong aspirations for work and career. The Australian Women's Working Futures Project shows that young women expect to be engaged in work over their life course in a similar pattern to young men (Baird et al. 2018). This aspiration for sustained participation in paid employment has been building for decades (see Figure 1.1), with labour market participation rates for women of all ages reaching a historic high of 62.4 per cent in 2022 and the retirement age of women increasing in a steady pattern (Gordon & Geraets 2023; Wade 2023b; KPMG 2022).

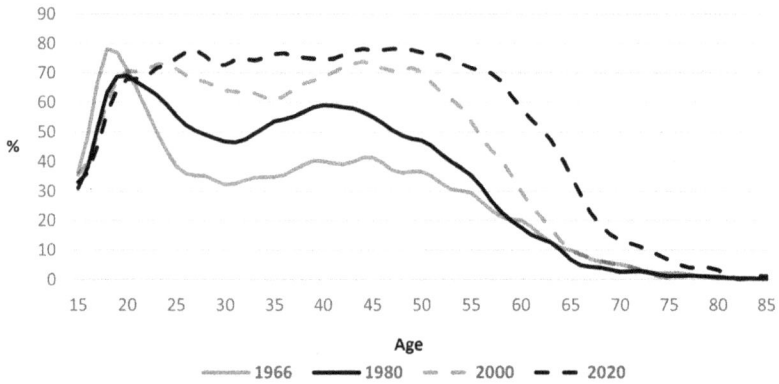

Figure 1.1 Employment-to-population ratio, females. Source: Australian Bureau of Statistics, 2021a, Labour Force Survey, Changing Female Employment over Time (18 March 2021)

Australian women are work and career oriented, and they aspire to jobs that pay well and in which they can be promoted. They value respect in the workplace, job security, flexibility, predictable hours, a measure of control and influence in the workplace, and work that makes a positive contribution to society (Hill et al. 2023; Hill et al. 2018; International Labour Organization 2017). Young Australian women are optimistic about the future of work in general and have the skills and drive to make a significant contribution to economic growth and productivity. However, a combination of highly segmented labour markets where women are concentrated in retail, education and caring occupations, the undervaluation of many of these highly feminised jobs, workplace disrespect and discrimination, and inadequate policy supports for workers with care responsibilities means Australian women dominate employment in part-time, low-wage and insecure forms of work (Foley & Cooper 2021). Platform or gig work is also growing and insecure, and casualised work is widespread – more so among women than men. In August 2022, 23.5 per cent of the total workforce were employed in casual positions, with 25.5 per cent of female workers in jobs that did not provide paid leave compared with 21.4 per cent of men (Australian Bureau of Statistics 2022).

4

The differences between women's and men's participation in paid work and the types of jobs they occupy is, in part, driven by social norms that continue to define women as primary carers and men as primary earners – norms which are reinforced by Australia's policy framework. Having a child delivers a boost in men's hours of work, whereas women's hours decline and never quite recover, with stark consequences for women's economic insecurity in old age (Bahar et al. 2022; Baird & Heron 2019). This mismatch between the demands of high-responsibility, secure and well-paid jobs, and family and community care roles is so significant that many young women express anxiety about the impact children will have on their hard-won career and economic security (Hill et al. 2019). Increasingly, young women are talking about not having children at all given the severity of the "motherhood penalty" they see colleagues face. Or they settle for one child only (Hill et al. 2019). This social shift is reflected in the fall in Australia's total fertility rate from 2.9 in 1970 to 1.7 in 2021, well below the replacement rate of 2.1 (Australian Bureau of Statistics 2021). Women who remain optimistic about their future identify key work and care reconciliation policies as critical to a successful future at work and in meeting their aspirations for family formation. Interestingly, young fathers are as likely as mothers to identify work and care policies like parental leave and affordable child care as essential to their future success at work (Hill et al. 2019) and there is increasing convergence between young men and women's expectations about work–family balance, even as it remains unmet (Hill et al. 2023).

Global debates about the "great resignation" (Goldberg 2022) and "quiet quitting" (Tapper 2022) have foregrounded a renewed desire by workers to find paid work that provides time and support for family care, hobbies and other personal interests. COVID-19 lockdowns showed employers and workers that work-from-home and other flexible working arrangements are possible and can contribute to worker wellbeing and workplace productivity. Some suggest that women stand to gain the most from new forms of flexible and hybrid working, as they will allow for better alignment between work and care (Baird & Dinale 2020). But there is a risk that more work-from-home could further entrench the gender division of labour and sideline women from accessing good jobs and promotion opportunities.

The post-COVID work-from-home debate highlights the stark gender inequalities that lie at the centre of the larger work and care policy debate. This debate, of course, ignores the many thousands of women who work in jobs that do not have the same options of working from home – for example, in medical and care services, teaching and frontline retail. This segmentation in work and opportunity reflects persistent labour market divisions, where women are concentrated in the occupations of health and education and men dominate construction, mining, transport, postal and warehousing and utilities (WGEA 2019: 5).

Decades of Australian research have shown how policy settings and social infrastructure funding have failed to transform gender inequalities in work and care, leaving households time poor and stressed as they try to patch together individual solutions to systemic problems. This was the focus of the first comprehensive assessment of the Australian work and care policy regime by Barbara Pocock, leading feminist workplace relations scholar and now Senator for South Australia. Published 20 years ago, the *Work/Life Collision* (2003) traces how changes in work and home life set families on a collision course in which the needs of the modern working household did not align with their care responsibilities and needs in other areas of life. The fallout, Pocock argued, is stress, a declining quality of life, time poverty, erosion of relationships, pressure on carers – especially women – and loss of community. Pocock's structural diagnosis of the problem points to policy failure and the need for governments to develop work and care systems that are fit for purpose and give families a chance to combine care with economic security. Two decades later, the need for a new policy architecture is starker than ever.

Since the release of Pocock's book, a rich scholarship has developed on policy limitations and failures of key work and care policies such as paid parental leave (Baird, et al. 2021; Baird & Murray 2014; Whitehouse et al. 2013), early childhood education and care (Hill & Wade 2018; Adamson & Brennan 2014; Hill et al. 2007), carers leave (Baird et al. 2022), right to request changes in working hours (Cooper & Baird 2015), respite services (Hamilton et al. 2016), the care workforce (Macdonald 2021; Charlesworth 2012) and care delivery models. This literature shows how Australia's peculiar hybrid system of publicly subsidised for-profit service delivery has failed to deliver both decent pay and conditions for the care workforce and high-quality care services for clients (Meagher et al. 2022; Macdonald 2021; Newberry & Brennan 2013; Meagher 2007).

Work–care policy has also become a regular feature of public and political debate among both experts and the community. The Australian Work + Family Policy Roundtable,[1] an academic network established in 2004, makes regular evidence-based contributions to the national debate through submissions to government inquiries and the publication of Federal Election Benchmarks on work, care and family policy. Since 2000, there has also been rapid growth in the number of businesses, civil society organisations and think tanks that have come to understand the social and economic importance of work and care policies and contributed new research evidence to the public debate. New broad-based coalitions of businesses, unions, academics and NGOs have flourished around campaigns for universal early childhood education and care, gender-equal parental leave and professional wages for care workers, reflecting changing community expectations (The Parenthood 2021; PricewaterhouseCoopers 2019; Thrive by Five 2017). The level of interest has seen some work and care policy issues, such as parental leave and flexible working, taken up by corporations who are running well ahead of government (UNICEF and Parents at Work 2022; Wittenberg-Cox 2021) even as they lag on early childhood education and care and elder care.

The work and care debate is also expanding, with new policy areas such as the reproductive health and wellbeing needs of workers and the transnational work and care arrangements of migrant workers gathering interest. In addition, concerns about declining fertility rates are gaining traction, with research showing that decisions about family formation are in part driven by the inadequacy of work and care policy settings (Hill et al. 2019). Pandemic lockdowns and restrictions on social interaction are expected to have a long-lasting negative impact on Australia's demographic profile (Allen 2020), with disruptions to labour markets, inflation and the persistence of high house prices also shaping young Australians' expectations about family formation. This

---

1   https://www.workandfamilypolicyroundtable.org.

takes the work and care policy debate into the centre of government concerns about the impact of declining fertility on economic prosperity and standard of living (Australian Government Centre for Population 2022; Australian Government 2021). We are at a critical turning point, and policy needs to take a new direction if Australian society is to be sustained.

1.3 A life course approach to work, care and family and the need for a new social contract that includes gender

A limitation of most work and care research is that it is focused on one moment in the life cycle, such as the birth of a new child, or on a particular sector of the care economy, such as aged care or early childhood education and care. In this book, we shift the frame to include the whole life course and the policies and care services that support workers and families from birth to the end of life. Everyone, at some stage of their life, requires care. Most of us, at some stage, are also required to provide care. But for generations, the social contract has simultaneously assumed and reinforced that it is women who are primarily responsible for care – with most of it supplied for free or very low wages. This is no longer acceptable, or even desirable. Post-pandemic labour markets mean that labour is in high demand and women's unemployment is at a historic low (Wade 2023a). Research from the Australian Women's Working Futures Project shows young men and women's expectations about combining work and care are converging, creating new challenges for employers and government policy (Hill et al. 2023; Baird et al. 2018).

Importantly, the giving and receiving of care is not limited to the birth of a young child or end of life. It is a daily, essential requirement. Australia's current policy architecture has too many breaks and schisms: between conception, birth and baby/infant care; between return to work and availability of care for children; between hours of work and school terms and times; and between career progression and the demands of elder care. It is usually assumed that women will cover these care gaps, which they have done for decades at great financial and personal cost.

The role of women as carers is so normalised within families, workplaces and public policy that it has become deeply internalised, with research showing women routinely express gratitude at having access to a "good boss" who understands the demands of family life, or a "good employer" who offers flexible working or part-time options (Probert 2002). This has not changed for decades. More recent research shows that women frequently talk about how "lucky" and "grateful" they are to be able to balance their work and care responsibilities, feeling like they have hit the "jackpot" or won the lottery when they are able to combine decent work with care (Cooper & Hill 2022). But luck should play no part in women's ability to combine paid work with family care. Care is essential to family and community life and is the foundation of a prosperous, productive economy. Workplace and public policies need to support, not punish, those with care responsibilities. A life course approach to policy development acknowledges the embeddedness of care in work and catalyses the development of a comprehensive policy framework that meets the needs of all people at each point in life when care needs are most acute.

A life course approach to work and care policy demands a new social contract – that is, a revised understanding of the policies and norms by which we live (Shafik 2021: xii) and, specifically in relation to work and care, a better understanding of the relations between women and men, between women and the state, and between women and their employers. In the new social contract, "luck" is replaced by intention, and positive work–care combinations are the result of good evidence-based policy design. If Australia can get the policy settings right, the benefits for families, workers, employers and governments will be immense, with worker wellbeing, gender equality, productivity and economic security enhanced. It is this possibility that causes us to rethink the structure and efficacy of current Australian work and care policies, how they have fared during the pandemic, and how they might be redesigned to deliver a new social contract in which everyone has both the capacity to work and the capacity to give and receive high-quality care in the manner that best suits them.

There is robust international evidence on what policies best support women and men to meet their aspirations for work and care and build economic security over the life course (UN Women 2018).

There is also detailed global evidence on what levels of public investment are needed to ensure that high-quality care services are delivered by a care workforce that enjoys professional recognition and decent wages (International Labour Organization 2022; International Labour Organization and UN Women 2021). But work and care policies cannot be left on a set-and-forget status. As the past few years have clearly demonstrated, health, economic and geopolitical crises can radically disrupt the work and care landscape – often without warning – driving rapid change in social needs and norms. Our policies need to be constantly monitored and updated to meet these evolving work and care needs and norms.

Most of us are worker/carers (Charlesworth & Macdonald 2017), and this reality must be reflected in a new social contract for Australian families. The social contract refers to the reciprocal relationship between the state and its citizens and can be defined as the policies and norms that regulate and govern how we live together or "what we owe each other" (Shafik 2021). In terms of paid work, the social contract sets out "the mutual expectations and obligations that workers, employers, and their communities and societies have regarding work and employment relationships" (Kochan & Dyer 2021: 25). Welfare policy scholars see the social contract as describing the metaphorical relationship between the state and its citizens, defining what citizens can expect in welfare support. During the second half of the 20th century, the neoliberal decades, this social contract came under pressure from governments that began to expect more of citizens in terms of their engagement in paid work in return for social services or welfare (Hamilton 2014), sometimes referred to as employment-based citizenship.

Interestingly, definitions of the social contract do not usually refer to gender. We argue, as feminist scholars, that embedded within the social contract is the "gender contract". In academic terms, the gender contract is "the systematic ordering of relations between women and men as a gender system that is constructed, controlled and reinforced by a gender-based power structure" (Haandrikman et al. 2019: 3). This refers to the explicitly gendered institutions and relations (such as marriage and motherhood) and the implicit norms that shape how men and women, boys and girls, relate to one another and the consequent structures of interdependency. In Australia, industrial relations institutions such as the "family wage" of the early 20th century set the terms of a deeply gendered social contract. In 1907, the Harvester Judgement determined the wage for an unskilled man be set at a level that would allow him to feed, clothe and house his wife and three children in "frugal comfort". In doing so, the law positioned men as breadwinners and women as homemakers, ensuring that men have benefited more than women from the employment relationship (Pateman 2014). The gendered nature of the family wage has continued to shape employment outcomes for women and men and contributed to the devaluing of women's work in the labour market. New labour laws and policies are aimed at changing this, but the task is immense.

Why is the gender contract important? As feminist political theorist Carole Pateman said some time ago, we live in an "employment society", where work is the marker of our citizenship and from which many economic and social benefits flow (Pateman 2014: 212). As public policies and welfare payments are increasingly linked to work and employment status, this is more so the case now than perhaps ever before. The gender contract at work is critical, therefore, because work is so central to our lives and our economy. We argue that the gender contract sits within the social contract and, for our purposes in this volume, refers to what we expect of women and men in terms of paid work and paid and unpaid care. In Australian workplaces today, we also need to broaden our understanding of the gender contract to be inclusive of not just cisgender men and women, but all people across the sex and gender spectrums, including those in transgender and non-binary communities. Furthermore, as research in Sweden has shown (Haandrikman et al. 2019), the gender contract can and does vary by geographic location, and any analysis of work and care also requires an intersectional approach that acknowledges class, race and age, ability, sexual orientation and gender identity (Folbre 2020).

In this book, we conceive of the social and gender contract in a broad manner that aligns with development economist Amartya Sen's capabilities framework and idea of wellbeing. Drawing on this tradition, the gender-social contract must be designed to enhance the capabilities of every person to live the type of life that they value at every stage of the life course, across diverse family and community settings. This means that resources such as income and care services must be provided within policy settings that enhance capabilities, opportunities and freedom to do and be what a person values (Sen 1999, 2009). In doing so, the capabilities of women to work and care are repositioned as central and not subservient to men's capabilities in these areas of life.

We need a new social and gender contract because the old one is redundant and broken. Profound changes in demography, education and women's expectations cut across and challenge prevailing social structures. The "ideal worker" norm of a full-time male breadwinner with a full-time wife as the homemaker is long dead. New policy architecture is required to build this new social contract, one that embeds a future-orientated long-term approach that sees care as an investment in sustained wellbeing and prosperity. As the ILO argues, a new social contract grounded in substantive gender equality, in which men and women have the right to give and receive high-quality care, could transform care labour from an individualised risk borne primarily by women into a social good that is recognised, redistributed and rewarded (International Labour Organization 2018). This would also shift the way care is delivered and the monetary and investment value placed on that care. As recent research shows, investment in social care infrastructure has "superior employment outcomes" for investment in other sectors, such as construction, improving employment rates and reducing gender employment gaps (De Henau & Himmelweit 2021: 454).

1.4 Our focus in this volume

Australia is at a critical turning point in work, care and family policy and, in this volume, we set out possible pathways towards a new and more equitable social and gender contract. Commonwealth, state and territory governments are making significant investments in policy innovations to drive women's economic opportunities, lift women's workforce participation and incentivise a more shared approach to unpaid care (Australian Government 2022; New South Wales Government 2022; South Australian Government 2022; Victorian

Government 2022). But there is more to be done. This volume draws on the most recent empirical evidence to show how a life course approach can be embedded within a new social and gender contract. Specifically, we evaluate five core aspects of Australia's work and care policy settings to ask: Where are we at, and where are we headed? We believe we are at a turning point where the opportunity to finally address the "work/life collision" (Pocock 2003) is before us.

Using the life course approach to provide the structure, the book begins with a chapter on reproductive support policies, an example of an evolving policy space that includes paid leave, benefits or flexible working arrangements for reproductive health concerns and interventions such as fertility treatments and pregnancy loss. This is followed by chapters on Australia's parental leave system and early childhood education and care. The book then moves to chapters on "good" and "bad" flexibility at work, and the policy framework for workers who have responsibilities for elder care and care for those with disability. We complete the book with a final chapter on the important question of income and expenditure, known as the tax and transfer system, and its implications for gender inequality in the distribution of work and care. Each of the chapters is written by experts in their field – academics who have thought deeply about and contributed to the debates about work and care policies in Australia.

In laying out a life course approach to the policy terms of a more equitable gender and social contract, we provide readers with an accessible and comprehensive account of how Australia has arrived at the current turning point, the rewards of making positive change, and possible ways to rebuild a fit-for-purpose work and care policy architecture that supports all people, regardless of age or gender, to give and receive care over the course of their working lives.

References

Adamson, E.A. and Brennan, D. (2014). Social investment or private profit? diverging notions of "investment" in early childhood education and care. *International Journal of Early Childhood* 46: 47–61.

Allen, L. (2020). COVID-19 could see thousands of women miss out on having kids, creating a demographic disaster for Australia. *The Conversation*, 20 July. https://bit.ly/3ZODoWJ.

Alon, T., Doepke, M., Olmstead-Rumsey, J. and Tertilt, M. (2020). *The Impact of COVID-19 on Gender Equality*. NBER Working Paper Series, Working Paper 26947. https://bit.ly/3NfvHUk.

Australian Bureau of Statistics (2022). *Working Arrangements*. https://bit.ly/47KeB9n.

Australian Government (2022). *Women's Budget Statement 2022–2023*. https://bit.ly/46Qnptl.

Australian Bureau of Statistics (2021). *Births, Australia*. Canberra: ABS. https://bit.ly/46NuQS2.

Australian Government (2021). *2021 Intergenerational Report*. Parkes, ACT: Department of the Treasury. https://bit.ly/3sZfADL.

Australian Government. (2017). *Towards 2025: An Australian Government Strategy to Boost Women's Workforce Participation*. Canberra: Department of Prime Minister and Cabinet.

Australian Government Centre for Population (2022). *Impacts of Policies on Fertility Rates*. https://bit.ly/46NuVFk.

Bahar, E., Bradshaw, N., Deutscher, N., and Montaigne, M. (2022). Children and the gender earnings gap. *Treasury Round Up*, October 2022. https://bit.ly/4abSnPb.

Baird, M., Cooper, R., Hill, E., Probyn, E. and Vromen, A. (2018). *Women and the Future of Work: Report 1 of the Australian Women's Working Futures Report*. University of Sydney. https://ses.library.usyd.edu.au/handle/2123/21254.

Baird, M. and Dinale, D. (2020). *Preferences for Flexible Working Arrangements: Before, During and After COVID-19*. Fair Work Commission. https://bit.ly/474oQo9.

Baird, M., Hamilton, M. and Constantin, V. (2021). Gender equality and paid parental leave in Australia: a decade of giant leaps or baby steps? *Journal of Industrial Relations* 63(4): 546–67.

Baird, M., Hamilton, M., Dinale, D., Gulesserian, L. and Heron, A. (2022). Broadening our conception of leave: leave to care for self or others over the life course. In I. Dobrotić, S. Blum and A. Koslowski, eds. *Research Handbook on Leave Policy*, 368–83. Cheltenham: Edward Elgar Publishing. https://doi.org/10.4337/9781800372214.

Baird, M. and Heron, A. (2019). The life cycle of women's employment in Australia and inequality markers. In R.D. Lansbury, A. Johnson and D. van dan Broek, eds. *Contemporary Issues in Work and Organisations: Actors and Institutions*, 42–56. Abingdon: Routledge.

Baird, M. and Murray, J. (2014). Collective bargaining for paid parental leave in Australia 2005–2010: a complex context effect. *The Economic Labour Relations Review* 25(1): 47-62.

Chapman, J., Skinner, N. and Pocock, B. (2014). Work–life interaction in the twenty-first century Australian workforce: five years of the Australian Work and Life Index. *Labour and Industry* 24(2): 87–102.

Charlesworth, S. (2012). Decent working conditions for care workers? The intersections of employment regulation, the funding market and gender norms. *Australian Journal of Labour Law* 25(2): 107–29.

Charlesworth, S. and Macdonald, F. (2017). Employment regulation and worker-carers: reproducing gender inequality in the domestic and market spheres? In D. Peetz and G. Murray, eds. *Women, Labor Segmentation and Regulation*, 79–96. New York: Palgrave Macmillan.

Charmes, J. (2019). *The unpaid care work and the labour market. An analysis of time use data based on the latest compilation of time-use surveys.* Geneva: International Labour Office. https://bit.ly/3RxY6aS.

Cooper, R. and Baird, M. (2015). Bringing the "right to request" flexible working arrangements to life: from policies to practices. *Employee Relations: The International Journal* 37(5): 568–81.

Cooper R., and Hill, E. (2022). *What do women want from work post-pandemic? A qualitative study of women in western Sydney.* Research report, Gender Equality in Working Life Research Initiative. Sydney: The University of Sydney.

Craig, L. and Churchill, B. (2021). Working and caring at home: gender differences in the effects of Covid-19 on paid and unpaid labour in Australia. *Feminist Economics* 27(1–2): 310–26.

Craig, L. and Sawrikar, P. (2009). Work and family: how does the (gender) balance change as children grow? *Gender, Work and Organization* 16(6): 684–709.

De Henau, J. and Himmelweit, S. (2021). A care-led recovery from COVID-19: investing in high-quality care to stimulate and rebalance the economy. *Feminist Economics* 27 (1–2): 453–69.

Folbre, N. (2020). *The Rise and Decline of Patriarchal Systems: An Intersectional Political Economy.* London: Verso.

Foley, M. and Cooper, R. (2021). Workplace gender equality in the post-pandemic era: where to next? *Journal of Industrial Relations* 63(4): 463–76.

Goldberg, E. (2022). Those job quitters during the great resignation? They're at work. *New York Times*, 13 May. https://bit.ly/45vDV1e.

Gordon, J. and Geraets, N. (2023). Melbourne workers waiting longer to retire than since the early '70s. *Sydney Morning Herald*, 23 February. https://bit.ly/48Hnd1B.

Haandrikman, K., Webster, N.A. and Duvander, A.Z. (2019). Understanding local variations in gender relations using gender contract theory. *Stockholm Research Reports in Demography*, 2019:06: 1–30.

Hamilton, M. (2014). The new social contract and the individualisation of risk in policy. *Journal of Risk Research* 17(4): 453–67.

Hamilton, M., Giuntoli, G., Johnson, K. and Fisher, K.R. (2016). *Transitioning Australian Respite*. UNSW Australia: Social Policy Research Centre Report 04/2016. https://bit.ly/3t7O86J.

Hill, E., Baird, M., Vromen, A., Cooper, R., Meers, Z. and Probyn, E. (2019). Young women and men: imagined futures of work and family formation in Australia. *Journal of Sociology* 55(4): 778–98.

Hill, E., Cooper, R., Baird, M., Vromen, A. and Probyn, E. (2018). *Australian Women's Working Futures: Are We Ready?* (pp. 1–27). Geneva, Switzerland: International Labour Organization. https://bit.ly/3t08GOD.

Hill, E., Cooper R., Vromen, A., Foley, M. and Seetahul, S. (2023). *Gender dynamics in the post-pandemic future of work. High level data release for International Women's Day 2023*. Research Note 1, Australian Women's Working Futures Project. The University of Sydney. https://doi.org/10.25910/20pf-4g85.

Hill, E., Pocock, B. and Elliott, A. (2007). *Kids Count: Better Early Childhood Education and Care in Australia*. Sydney: Sydney University Press.

Hill, E. and Wade, M. (2018). "The radical marketisation" of early childhood education and care in Australia. In D. Cahill and P. Toner, eds. *Wrong Way: How Privatisation and Economic Reform Backfired*, 21–39. Carlton: La Trobe University Press in conjunction with Black Inc.

International Labour Organization (2022). *Care at Work: Investing in Care Leave and Services for a More Gender Equal World of Work*. https://bit.ly/3Nhnjno.

International Labour Organization (2021). *Policy Brief: An Uneven and Gender-unequal COVID-19 Recovery: Update on Gender and Employment Trends 2021*. https://bit.ly/46NWa2k.

International Labour Organization (2018). *Care Work and Care Jobs for the Future of Decent Work*. https://bit.ly/46TCKsW.

International Labour Organization (2017). *Towards a Better Future for Women and Work: Voices of Women and Men*. https://bit.ly/47NitXd.

International Labour Organization and UN Women (2021). *A guide to public investments in the care economy. Policy support tool for estimating care deficits, investment costs and economic returns*. https://bit.ly/3RgSyQP.

Kochan, T.A. and Dyer, L. (2021). *Shaping the future of work: a handbook for action and a new social contract*. New York: Routledge.

KPMG (2022). *When will I retire?* https://bit.ly/47NKP3N.

Macdonald, F. (2021) *Individualising Risk: Paid Care Work in the New Gig Economy*. Singapore: Palgrave Macmillan.

Macdonald, F., Malone, J. and Charlesworth, S. (2020). *Women, work, care and COVID*. School of Management, RMIT University. https://bit.ly/3NhKkqe.

Meagher, G. (2007). The challenge of the care workforce: recent trends and emerging problems. *Australian Journal of Social Issues* 42(2): 151–67.

Meagher G., Stebbing. A., and Perche, D., eds. (2022) *Designing Social Service Markets: Risk, regulation and rent-seeking*. Canberra: ANU Press.

Newberry, S and Brennan D, (2013). The marketisation of early childhood education and care (ECEC) in Australia: a structured response. *Financial Accountability and Management* 29(3): 227–45. https://doi.org/10.1111/faam.12018.

New South Wales Government (2022). *NSW Budget 2022–23: Overview*. https://bit.ly/47MdOVD.

OECD (2021). *Caregiving in Crisis: Gender Inequality in Paid and Unpaid Work during COVID-19*. https://bit.ly/3trniX6.

The Parenthood (2021). *Making Australia the Best Place in the World to be a Parent*. https://bit.ly/46lunqJ.

Pateman, C. (2014) *The Sexual Contract*. Hoboken: Wiley.

Patty, A. and Wade, M. (2021). This lockdown, women are once again doing more of the housework, home schooling. *Sydney Morning Herald*, 31 July. https://bit.ly/3PLWb0b.

Pocock, B. (2003). *The Work/Life Collision: What Work is Doing to Australians and What to do about it*. Annandale, NSW: Federation Press.

Pocock, B., Skinner, N. and Williams, P. (2012). *Time Bomb: Work, Rest and Play in Australia Today*. Sydney: University of New South Wales Press.

Pricewaterhouse Coopers (2019). *A Smart Investment for a Smarter Australia: Economic Analysis of Universal Early Childhood Education in the Year Before School in Australia*. https://bit.ly/3RfTBjO.

Probert, B. (2002). "Grateful slaves" or "self-made women": a matter of choice or policy? *Australian Feminist Studies* 17(37): 7–17.

Sen, A (2009). *The Idea of Justice*. London: Allen Lane.

Sen, A. (1999). *Development as Freedom*. New York: Alfred Knopf.

Shafik, M. (2021). *What we owe each other: A new social contract*. London: The Bodley Head.

South Australian Government (2022). *Royal Commission into Early Childhood Education & Care*. https://www.royalcommissionecec.sa.gov.au/.

Tapper, J. (2022). Quiet quitting: why doing the bare minimum at work has gone global. *The Guardian*, 6 August. https://bit.ly/4a84P2C.

Thrive By Five (2017). *Time to Act: Investing in Our Children and Our Future.* https://bit.ly/4a2MtzU.

UN Women (2021). *Women and Girls Left Behind: Glaring Gaps in Pandemic Responses.* https://bit.ly/3RbQitV.

UN Women (2020). Whose time to care: unpaid care and domestic work during COVID-19. Policy brief. https://bit.ly/4a4F5nP.

UN Women (2018). *Promoting Women's Economic Empowerment: Recognizing and Investing in the Care Economy.* https://bit.ly/4acR6HA.

UN Women and UNDP (2022). *Government Responses to COVID-19: Lessons on gender equality for a world in turmoil.* https://bit.ly/3Q4u5i9.

UNICEF and Parents at Work (2022). *Bridging the Work and Family Divide: Understanding the Benefits of Family Friendly Workplaces.* https://bit.ly/486Pcq6.

Victorian Government (2022). *Victorian Budget 22/23: Ready for school. Early years investment to support strong foundational education.* https://www.vic.gov.au/victorian-budget-department-education#early-childhood-education.

Wade, M. (2023a). NSW women's jobless rate hits record low – beating the outcome for men. *Sydney Morning Herald*, 26 February. https://bit.ly/46oENG0.

Wade, M. (2023b). Why Sydneysiders are working longer than ever. *Sydney Morning Herald*, 23 February. https://bit.ly/3NmKP2n.

WGEA (2019). Gender segregation in Australia's workforce. Factsheet Series. https://bit.ly/3NjXDGS.

Whitehouse, G., Hewitt, B., Martin, B. and Baird, M. (2013). Employer-paid maternity leave in Australia: a comparison of uptake and duration in 2005 and 2010. *Australian Journal of Labour Economics* 16(3): 311–27.

Wittenberg-Cox, A. (2021). Flexibility for all: Unilever's vision of the future of work. *Forbes*, 23 May. https://bit.ly/3GxfpCz.

Work + Family Policy Roundtable (2022) *Work, Care & Family Policies: Federal Election Benchmarks 2022.* https://bit.ly/3GxfrdF.

Work + Family Policy Roundtable (2020). *Work + care in a gender inclusive recovery: A bold policy agenda for a new social contract.* https://bit.ly/3RziatE.

2
Reproductive policies: An expanding approach to work and care

Sydney Colussi, Elizabeth Hill and Marian Baird

2.1 Introduction

Workplace policies to support the reproductive body have not been part of the regular compendium of work–care policy areas to date. However, as younger and older women's labour market engagement grows, and fertility declines, reproductive policies are emerging as an important new part of the work, care and family policy architecture in Australia and internationally. The term reproductive policies covers a broad spectrum of workplace policies and initiatives that provide people with paid leave, benefits or flexible working arrangements for a range of reproductive health concerns including menstruation, pregnancy loss, fertility treatments and menopause. This policy area has been the subject of considerable global interest and debate over the past five years, with governments and employers in Australia, India, Ireland, Malta, New Zealand, Spain and the United Kingdom – to name just a few – introducing new reproductive policies. Trade unions have also been advocating and bargaining for workplace reproductive policies to address workplace constraints on reproductive wellbeing and to help people work and care for their bodies over the life course.

Reproductive policies challenge old notions of the "ideal" (cisgender male) worker as body-less and care-less, giving way to a more realistic understanding of workers, their reproductive bodies and responsibilities. Important social, demographic and technological shifts are behind these changing attitudes, particularly among women and young people, and help explain the rising popularity of this policy area. To date, work–care policies have not adequately supported family formation, instead penalising the careers of young people, especially young women, who have children. Australian women, and women in most high-income countries, are increasingly deferring or opting out of parenthood because the costs are "too high" under existing limited workplace supports for care, such as parental leave and child care (Hill et al. 2019: 794). This is reflected in Australia's declining fertility rate, which has been below the replacement level of 2.1 babies per woman since 1976 and is currently under 1.8 (Australian Bureau of Statistics 2021a, 2021b). This trend corresponds with a shift towards later child-bearing, which has spurred demand for assisted reproductive technologies (ARTs). In 2019, it was estimated that 4.9% of all women who gave birth in Australia received ART treatment, with 81,049 ART cycles reported from Australian clinics in 2019 (Newman et al. 2021: 1–4).

Dissatisfaction with the status quo has seen reproductive policies gaining traction with governments, companies, unions and women's groups as a new area of gender-responsive policy. The changing expectations and attitudes of women workers align with a growing body of research evidence on poor workplace supports for menstruation (Karin 2022; Golding & Hvala 2021), fertility treatment (Hvala 2018), pregnancy loss (Rose & Oxlad 2022; Meunier et al. 2021) and menopause (Beck, Brewis & Davies 2021; Brewis et al. 2017). Inadequate recognition and support for these reproductive concerns have been found to contribute to inequality and gendered disadvantage at work, with some women reporting reduced wellbeing and economic participation (Munro 2022; Barrington et al. 2021; Schoep et al. 2019), discrimination (Goldblatt & Steele 2019) and withdrawal from the labour market (British Medical Association 2020). This chapter examines a range of reproductive policies and considers their ability to deliver work–care reconciliation for people of different ages in Australia across the life course. This new policy domain challenges male-oriented workplace norms and practices that overlook the reproductive body and the unpaid work and care that is needed to maintain the body and its connection to the labour market over time. The chapter begins with a discussion of the history and context of reproductive policies in Australia, before providing an overview of the current policy architecture. This discussion shows this is an emerging policy area and there is not yet a cohesive legislative framework for these issues, but rather a patchwork of government and employer-provided entitlements. The chapter then considers policy debates and tensions that arise about the reproductive body before exploring potential avenues for change. A life course approach to the body is adopted and for this reason the chapter focuses on menstruation, fertility treatments, pregnancy loss and menopause as important reproductive (and post-reproductive) health concerns that require attention from policymakers. These are also receiving the greatest attention from employers, government and unions at present. Pregnancy, childbirth and parenthood are not covered in this chapter because workplace supports for these issues already exist and are addressed under the policy architecture for parental leave (see Chapter 3).

2.2 Reproductive policies in Australia: History and context

In a global sense, workplace policies for reproductive wellbeing are not new. Since the early 20th century, many countries across various regions and stages of economic development have implemented workplace policies and labour legislation to accommodate the reproductive body (Baird, Hill & Colussi 2021). These were focused primarily on paid leave for menstruation. In Australia, reproductive policy emerged as an industrial issue in the early 2000s when unions brought claims for menstrual leave at the University of Sydney in 2003 and at Toyota Australia in 2005.

Both claims were controversial. The policy at the University of Sydney had the support of the National Tertiary Education Union but was accused of perpetuating gender stereotypes and discriminating against men (Denholm 2003; Walker 2003). The efforts of the Australian Manufacturing Workers' Union to have menstrual leave introduced at Toyota were also criticised by employers, who argued it would reduce productivity and raise interest rates by increasing the cost of labour (*ABC News* 2005; Pryor and AAP 2005; *Sydney Morning Herald* 2005). Importantly, both unions argued there was a need for dedicated paid leave because "menstruation is not a sickness, it is just simply part of being a woman" (Balogh 2005).

In the early 2000s, reproductive policies were specifically focused on the needs of cisgender women. In recent years, the approach to reproductive policies has shifted and they are more likely to recognise and accommodate the health and wellbeing needs of transgender, non-binary and gender fluid people. This change is also reflected in the rise of paid gender affirmation leave in some enterprise agreements and employer policies in Australia (Silva 2022; Whittard 2021). Despite these developments and growing interest in this policy area among government and employers, few reproductive benefits have been formally integrated into Australian legislation and public policy. Most policy innovation is occurring in the private sector.

2.3 Current policy architecture

Much of the current policy architecture for the reproductive body is focused on paid leave, which can be divided into three categories. First, there are entitlements in federal legislation for personal or "sick" leave that may cover workplace absences related to menstruation, pregnancy loss, fertility treatment or menopause but are not designed to specifically accommodate these issues. Second, there are entitlements for miscarriage and stillbirth that are embedded in the policy architecture for parental leave. Third, there are special-purpose policies, usually offered by private employers but sometimes by state or territory governments, that are targeted at specific reproductive health concerns.

Entitlements in federal legislation

Personal ("sick") and carers leave

The National Employment Standards of the *Fair Work Act 2009* (Cth) provide all eligible national system employees[1] with up to 10 days paid leave each year for personal (or "sick") and carers leave (Golding 2021). Casuals are excluded and instead receive a wage loading intended to compensate for the lack of paid leave (Markey & McIvor 2018). The COVID-19 pandemic exposed the flaws of this system when many casual workers were left without pay while in forced isolation (Foley & Cooper 2021). Under s 97 of the *Fair Work Act*, an employee can claim personal/carers leave in two circumstances: if the employee is not fit for work because of a personal illness or injury affecting the employee; or to care for a family or household member because of a personal illness, injury or unexpected emergency affecting that person. An employer can request evidence, such as a medical certificate, to show the leave was taken for one of these reasons.

The current policy architecture for personal/carers leave creates practical challenges for those who require leave to care for their reproductive bodies. First, eligibility for the benefit, in particular what constitutes an "illness" or "injury" under the *Fair Work Act*, is a source of ongoing debate and confusion. Although stress and pregnancy-related illnesses have been identified as falling within the scope of the benefit, there is "minimal authoritative guidance" on other conditions that may satisfy the illness or injury requirement (Golding & Hvala 2021: 356). This means some reproductive (and post-reproductive) health concerns, such as menstruation, fertility treatment and menopause, may not be covered. For example, a woman may be eligible to claim personal leave if she is receiving in-vitro fertilisation treatment that requires anaesthesia, but non-invasive fertility treatment or consultations may not be a legitimate reason for taking personal leave (Hvala 2018: 914). Similarly, severe menstrual pain caused by endometriosis, a chronic gynaecological condition, is more likely to satisfy the illness or injury requirement than period pain that falls below the clinical threshold of a menstrual "disorder" (Golding & Hvala 2021: 356).

There is also the fundamental challenge of workers taking "sick" leave for essential or unavoidable bodily functions like menstruation or

---

1   A "national system employee" is anyone who is employed by a "national system employer" that is bound by national workplace relations laws under s 14 of the *Fair Work Act* (Fair Work Commission 2022).

menopause. This approach reflects a policy framework that caters to the needs of an ideal (cisgender male) worker who is assumed to not have reproductive health concerns. It also reinforces stigma about innate facets of female biology and indirectly discriminates against cisgender women and non-binary and gender fluid people, who are more likely than men to require extra leave to care for their reproductive bodies (Golding & Hvala 2021: 356; Goldblatt & Steele 2019: 306). Furthermore, research shows women often conserve their personal leave for child or aged care obligations (see Chapters 4 and 6), leaving them without enough leave for their own reproductive health concerns, such as fertility treatments and pregnancy loss (Hvala 2018: 916; Australian Human Rights Commission 2014: 90).

Leave for pregnancy loss

Statutory entitlements for miscarriage and stillbirth are found in both the *Fair Work Act* and the *Paid Parental Leave Act 2010* (Cth). These benefits include special maternity leave for pregnancy-related illnesses or miscarriage, compassionate leave for miscarriage, and unpaid or paid parental leave for stillbirth (see Table 2.1). These policies offer important protections, but the current policy architecture does not deliver work–care reconciliation for all people. For example, some policies do not cover pregnancy loss at earlier stages of gestation (Rose & Oxlad 2022: 280) and abortion is not included as a ground for compassionate leave under the *Fair Work Act*, which risks reinforcing the idea that some types of pregnancy loss are more deserving of leave. Several of these benefits are also unpaid and, as a result, may not offer grieving parents enough economic security following pregnancy loss. Finally, as this policy area is geared towards cisgender women and heterosexual couples, research shows there is often not enough support for fathers (Obst et al. 2020) and parents in the LGBTQ+ community (Rose & Oxlad 2022). These issues have prompted calls for more tailored policy responses and flexibility to recognise that "people experience pregnancy loss in unique ways and have individual physical, psychological and emotional needs, capacities and coping strategies" (Rose & Oxlad 2022: 280).

Employer entitlements

Most of the innovation in reproductive policy is occurring in the private sector rather than within federal legislation (see Table 2.2), including new leave types, designs and alternative workplace arrangements. While some employers are introducing policies for menstruation and menopause leave, others are developing more flexible and bespoke approaches to workplace management or packaging together leave for fertility treatments and miscarriage with parental leave to create "family formation" bundles (Aubrey 2021). At the employer level, parental and reproductive policies are merging as employer efforts to improve parental benefits for pregnancy and child care overlap with new policies to accommodate a wider range of reproductive (and post-reproductive) health concerns.

Menstruation and menopause policies

In May 2016, the Victorian Women's Trust, a gender equity organisation, made global headlines for introducing a high-profile menstruation and menopause policy – one of the first to be introduced by an Australian employer since the early 2000s. The policy allows any menstruating or menopausal employee to work from home, request flexible working arrangements or claim a day of monthly paid leave without a medical certificate (Victorian Women's Trust 2021). Other employers have since followed and implemented their own policies. In January 2021, Future Super, an ethical superannuation company, introduced six days paid leave and flexible working arrangements for menstruation and menopause, with no medical certificate required (Shams 2021). In May 2021, Modibodi, a period and incontinence underwear brand, introduced 10 days paid leave for menstruation and menopause and included miscarriage as an additional ground for leave (Nelson 2021).

Table 2.1 Pregnancy loss in federal legislation

Entitlement	Length	Payment	Scope	Eligibility	Notice and evidence	Legislation
Special maternity leave (Fair Work Ombudsman 2022c)	Until the employee is fit for work	Unpaid	Pregnancy-related illness or miscarriage after at least 12 weeks gestation	All national system female employees with 12 months continuous service and "regular" casuals with 12 months continuous service.	Must provide notice and indication of expected period of leave. If required by employer, must provide evidence (e.g., medical certificate).	*Fair Work Act* ss 67, 80
Unpaid parental leave (Fair Work Ombudsman 2022b, 2022c)	Up to 12 months, with the option to request an additional 12 months leave in writing	Unpaid	Stillbirth (weighs at least 400 grams at delivery or 20 weeks gestation)	All national system employees (including "regular" casuals) with at least 12 months continuous service.	Must provide written notice 10 weeks before starting the leave, or as soon as practicable. If required by employer, must provide evidence (e.g., medical certificate).	*Fair Work Act* ss 70–72, 74, 77A
Compassionate leave (Fair Work Ombudsman 2022a)	Two days leave each time eligibility criteria are met	Paid for full-time and part-time national system employees, unpaid for casuals	Miscarriage (loss of pregnancy before 20 weeks) or stillbirth	All national system employees (including casuals) are eligible if they or their partner has a miscarriage or if the child is stillborn. Eligible employees may claim this benefit while on unpaid parental leave.	Must provide notice and indication of expected period of leave. If requested by employer, may have to provide evidence (e.g., statutory declaration).	*Fair Work Act* ss 104, 107
Paid parental leave (PPL)	18 weeks (PPL) and	Paid	Stillbirth (weighs at least 400 grams	Part 2–3 of the *Paid Parental Leave Act*: work	See Chapter 3 in this volume	*Paid Parental*

Entitlement	Length	Payment	Scope	Eligibility	Notice and evidence	Legislation
and Dad and Partner Pay (DaPP) (Obst et al. 2020)	2 weeks (DaPP)		at delivery or 20 weeks gestation)	test (div 3), income test (div 4), Australian residency test (div 5)		*Leave Act* ss 31, 31AA, 277, 115CB

At each of these employers, the policy was explicitly designed to normalise and de-stigmatise menstruation and menopause (Bell 2021) and enable employees to self-care, ensuring they do not expend sick leave on a "completely natural health reality" (Melican & Mountford 2017). Business reasons are also driving this change. Policymakers within these employers acknowledge the reputational benefits of gender-inclusive practices, which help to attract and retain staff, and have reported increased engagement and productivity among women workers and improved trust between employees and managers as a result of their implementation. These benefits are viewed by managers as outweighing the financial costs, which in practice have not been high as few eligible employees reportedly claim the full benefit (Francis 2022; Muroi 2022).

Family formation and pregnancy loss policies

Another shift is the expansion and combination of parental leave with fertility benefits and bereavement leave for pregnancy loss, sometimes referred to as "family formation" (Aubrey 2021) or "becoming a parent" policy bundles (Ahwan 2022). Some Australian employers, such as financial technology company Zip Co, have introduced bereavement leave for miscarriage as a stand-alone policy to create more inclusive working conditions for grieving parents (see Table 2.2). However, it is more common for employers to introduce benefits for pregnancy loss in conjunction with other related policies such as parental leave and paid leave or flexible work for fertility treatments like in-vitro fertilisation (IVF) or egg freezing. For example, in July 2021, global law firm Ashurst introduced a new global parental leave policy that includes two weeks paid leave for pregnancy loss and five days paid leave for fertility treatments. This policy is similar to one offered by the Asia–Pacific branch of music-streaming platform Spotify, which includes six months paid parental leave and a generous monetary allowance for IVF treatments, donor services and fertility preservation (Aubrey 2021). Harrison.ai, an Australian health tech company, has a comparable policy bundle that includes up to AU$10,000 for fertility treatments, 16 weeks paid leave for pregnancy loss and 16 weeks paid parental leave (Ahwan 2022).

Table 2.2 Reproductive policies in Australian private sector 2016–2022

Year	Employer	Industry	Reproductive concern	Policy design
2016	Victorian Women's Trust (2021)	Gender equity organisation	Menstruation and menopause	Work from home, flexible working arrangements or 1 day paid leave per month
2020	Commonwealth Bank of Australia (2020)	Financial institution	Pregnancy loss	Parental leave expanded to include stillbirth
2020	Repromed (Australian Nursing and Midwifery Federation 2020)	Fertility clinic	Fertility treatment	Paid leave for IVF treatments
2021	Zip Co (2021)	Financial technology	Pregnancy loss	Paid bereavement leave for miscarriage before 20 weeks
2021	Future Super (Prasser 2021)	Ethical superannuation company	Menstruation and menopause	6 days paid leave and flexible working arrangements
2021	Modibodi (Nelson 2021)	Sustainable period underwear brand	Menstruation, menopause and miscarriage	10 days paid leave
2021	Ashurst (2021)	Law firm	Pregnancy loss and fertility treatments	Parental leave package includes 2 weeks paid leave for pregnancy loss and 5 days paid leave for fertility treatments
2021	Spotify (Aubrey 2021)	Music-streaming platform	Fertility treatments	Parental leave package includes lifetime allowance for IVF, donor services and fertility preservation

Year	Employer	Industry	Reproductive concern	Policy design
2022	Harrison.ai (Ahwan 2022)	Health technology company	Pregnancy loss and fertility treatments	Parental leave package includes $10,000 for egg and sperm collection and IVF and 16 weeks paid leave for pregnancy loss

Trade unions and bargaining

Trade unions are also beginning to take a leading role in advancing reproductive leave in enterprise bargaining. In 2015, 35 hours of paid IVF leave was incorporated in the enterprise agreement of the Police Association of Victoria (Robertson 2017; Bucci & Willingham 2015). According to Police Association representatives, the purpose of the benefit was to ensure workers did not expend their personal leave on this issue and to "recognise IVF leave in the same mould as prenatal leave" (Robertson 2017: 39). In 2016, a similar benefit was included in the enterprise agreement of the Alpine Shire Council in Victoria (Hvala 2018: 936). In February 2020, the Health and Community Services Union in Victoria entered a ground-breaking claim for "Reproductive Health and Wellbeing Leave" in its enterprise agreement for mental health workers. The original claim was for five days paid leave and flexible working arrangements for a wide range of reproductive health and wellbeing issues including menstruation, menopause, fertility treatments, hysterectomies, vasectomies, miscarriages, terminations and gender affirmation (Tuohy 2020). The rationale behind the claim was to improve working conditions for women and transgender and non-binary people, who are more likely to "use up" their leave on these issues, and to tackle the taboo of reproductive health in the workplace (Health and Community Services Union 2020). Reproductive leave was also framed as an important means of achieving work–care reconciliation and as complementary to other policies in this area such as parental leave, child care and flexible work (see Chapters 3–5). While the original clause was opposed and ultimately rejected by employers, this was a world-first attempt to give such a diverse range of reproductive issues their own status in an enterprise agreement (Baird, Hill & Colussi 2022). The Health and Community Services Union campaign has sparked interest in the idea of reproductive policy within the union movement, particularly within the health sector.

Between 2020 and 2022, several unions in the feminised education sector introduced and bargained for reproductive policies, with a focus on benefits for menstruation and menopause. In November 2020, the Queensland Teachers' Union announced a pilot program to become a "menopause friendly" organisation and improve working conditions for women, which involved amending the Queensland Teachers' Union flexible work policy to allow staff to request flexible hours and workplace adjustments for menopause (Muldowney 2021; Queensland Teachers' Union 2020: 18). Mirroring its involvement with this policy area in the early 2000s, the New South Wales and Northern Territory branches of the National Tertiary Education Union brought claims for menstruation and menopause leave in their bargaining with the University of Sydney and Charles Darwin University in 2022. At the University of Sydney, the claim was settled as part of an extended personal leave clause rather than as a separate leave policy.

State government policies and regulations

New policies have also been introduced by some state governments. In 2021–22, the New South Wales government implemented reproductive leave benefits for pregnancy loss and fertility treatments, making it the first state in Australia to introduce policies of this kind. In June 2021, it was announced that all full-time and part-time workers in the public sector would be granted five days paid bereavement leave for miscarriage and stillbirth, with then NSW Treasurer Dominic Perrottet saying, "having a miscarriage is not an illness; it is a loss that should be recognised" (Hislop 2021). In May 2022, the NSW government announced an "Affordable IVF initiative" as part of the 2022–23 Budget that extended five days paid fertility treatment leave to teachers, nurses and other public sector workers. This initiative also included a $2,000 fertility treatment rebate and a $500 pre-IVF fertility testing rebate for NSW residents who have undergone eligible fertility tests or medical procedures at accredited clinics, and fertility preservation services for patients with cancer or other medical needs (New South Wales Health 2022). In June 2022, the NSW government announced a further $40 million in funding for specialist menopause health services and a state-wide education campaign for GPs and employers on menopause symptoms (Cormack 2022). This investment package did not offer menopause leave for public sector workers, but the potential impact of menopause on the economic security of women was acknowledged. Although New South Wales was the first and, so far, the only state or territory to offer these benefits, the former federal Coalition government under Prime Minister Scott Morrison also turned its attention to reproductive health in the lead-up to the federal election in May 2022, earmarking $58 million in 2022–23 for endometriosis services in recognition of the impact on women's health, education and employment (Read 2022). Introduction of this group of reproductive health policies signals government interest in new ways to support women's workforce participation and family formation.

2.4 Current debates and tensions

Reproductive policy is gaining traction in Australia in the context of declining fertility rates, increasing participation of women in paid employment and changing social attitudes towards gender and reproduction. However, the existing policy architecture for these issues does not afford people enough time, flexibility or protection to care for their reproductive bodies. While some Australians have access to reproductive policies through an enterprise agreement or employer policy, most do not and there are few legislative protections in place. There are also unresolved debates about the need for reproductive leave, with disagreement between those who think policy will deliver gender equality at work and those who argue specialist benefits will undermine women's employment by increasing the cost of female labour and perpetuating negative stereotypes. This goes to the important question of whether bodily functions like menstruation and menopause should be accommodated under "sick" leave or dedicated leave policies. These are critical tensions that will shape the design, implementation and impact of reproductive leave.

Design

As an emerging policy area with limited data on best practice approaches, how to effectively design reproductive policies, particularly paid leave, is not yet clear. An overarching question is how to categorise workplace leaves and benefits for different bodily functions. Given the link between reproductive capacity and gender discrimination, some feminist scholars argue that special measures like menstruation or menopause leave could reinforce rather than remedy gender inequality in the workplace by strengthening the harmful idea that women are weak, more expensive and less capable of paid work than men (Baird, Hill & Colussi 2021; King 2021; Goldblatt & Steele 2019). This suggests that a gender-neutral approach, in which governments and employers simply expand "sick" leave to cover all reproductive health concerns, may be preferable. However, as discussed above, this approach indirectly discriminates against women and non-binary and gender fluid people, who are more likely than men to require additional leave for their reproductive health or caring obligations.

There is also the issue of language and representation in the design of policies. Categorising menstruation or menopause as illnesses under the current policy architecture not only mischaracterises these innate functions but also pathologises the female body relative to the ideal male worker norm (Golding & Hvala 2021). Similar challenges arise in relation to pregnancy loss. As discussed above, leave for miscarriage or stillbirth rather than pregnancy loss could exclude women who require support following an abortion (Colussi, Hill & Baird 2022). Heteronormative and cisgendered assumptions about family formation and parenthood, such as the provision of maternity and paternity rather than parental leave, may undermine the ability of people in the LGBTQ+ community to access leave for pregnancy loss (Rose & Oxlad 2022: 13). There is also an argument that leave for pregnancy loss should be offered as bereavement leave rather than parental leave in recognition of the grief associated with this type of loss (Rose & Oxlad 2022: 276; Obst et al. 2020). Finally, it is important that the reproductive health needs and responsibilities of men are included in policies like paid leave for IVF and pregnancy loss, to recognise that both men and women have an important role in fertility management and family formation.

Developing an appropriate model for reproductive leave, including duration, payment and eligibility requirements, is another policy design challenge. For example, in some cases reproductive leave may not be as beneficial to workers as reproductive flexibility for uncertain or prolonged processes like fertility treatment or menopause (see Chapter 5). This approach may help to avoid an essentialist view of these issues by acknowledging that people do not experience them in the same way; some people may require formal workplace supports while others may not require or desire any at all (King 2021). In terms of remuneration, paid leave protects the economic security of workers who need to forgo income to care for their reproductive bodies, but reasonable requests for unpaid leave should also be allowed (Hvala 2018). To avoid imposing an additional burden on workers who may already be experiencing physical or emotional distress, eligibility and evidence requirements should be flexible or suspended in some cases, particularly for chronic and under-diagnosed conditions like endometriosis, for which many people struggle to obtain medical documentation (Young et al. 2015).

Implementation

How to successfully implement reproductive policy is another critical tension. If these policies are to deliver work–care reconciliation for all people, they must be responsive to changes in the body over the life course and also to the reproductive needs and activities of a diverse workforce. This means the practical application of reproductive policies must be shaped by the context in which they are implemented, including different sectors, occupations and workplaces, as well as the specific needs of individual workers. Most of the employer-provided benefits discussed in this chapter have been implemented in sectors like law, technology, finance and education where workers may have more predictable schedules and working environments compared to other sectors, like health care, where shift work, long hours and under-staffing may complicate the implementation of reproductive leave. Health care, as a feminised sector with workforce sustainability issues, may have a more acute need for these policies, but it may be more challenging to deliver beneficial outcomes to workers in these contexts. There is also the important question of who bears the cost of paid reproductive leave, for example, employers or taxpayers.

There are also important concerns regarding privacy and disclosure, which are problems for both workers and employers. For example, if menstrual leave requires supervisor approval, this could be harmful for non-binary and gender fluid people, who may not wish to discuss their gender identity at work, or for Aboriginal and Torres Strait Islander employees, who may not wish to disclose their menstrual status due to the cultural protocol of "Women's Business" (Munro 2022: 34). These issues underscore the complexity of this policy area and the need for an intersectional lens to be applied in developing these policies to accommodate the reproductive needs and activities of different groups (Goldblatt & Steele 2019). These concerns also help to explain the growing popularity of "living life" (Baird et al. 2022) or "life leave" (*HR Daily* 2022) policies that are available to workers for any personal or health concerns without the requirement to disclose why leave is being taken.

Another fundamental challenge is introducing and aligning law and policy reform with community, organisational and cultural change. Formally implementing reproductive leave does not mean a positive shift in attitudes will necessarily follow. The literature shows that menstruation and menopause are taboo subjects in the workplace, with many women unwilling to request workplace adjustments or leave due to a fear of discrimination (Atkinson et al. 2020; Grandey et al. 2020). Historical and contemporary evidence shows that menstruation has been a source of workplace discrimination in high-income countries, including Australia, and may be used to justify the exclusion of women from some male-dominated occupations, such as airline pilots (Goldblatt & Steele 2019: 304). In a growing number of court and tribunal cases in New Zealand, South Korea, the United Kingdom and the United States, workers are alleging discrimination and unfair treatment in relation to menstruation and menopause (see Filmer 2022; *BBC News* 2021; Hill 2021). At the same time, there has been increasing recognition of the unique challenges faced by transgender and gender diverse menstruators, who navigate the risks of both menstrual stigma and transphobia in the workplace (Atkins 2020). Pregnancy loss and fertility treatment may also be silenced in professional settings, with the available literature showing there is a lack of education and awareness within organisations about these issues and their potential impact on individual wellbeing and capacity to work (Hvala 2018; McCarthy et al. 2018; Porschitz & Siler 2017; Australian Human Rights Commission 2014). The rollout of reproductive policies may need accompanying education and training to ensure managers understand and are aware of the purpose of these benefits.

Evaluation and impact

Reproductive policy is, in many ways, a new and exciting concept, but it is also under-evaluated. The ability of these policies to deliver work–care reconciliation or gender equality is not yet clear and more research is needed on the impact of different models on workers and workplaces. While there is anecdotal evidence from some Australian employers on the benefits of these policies, there is little unbiased or peer-reviewed data on the estimated costs, rates of uptake and managerial and employee attitudes towards these policies. Addressing this gap in knowledge is essential if policymakers are to justify the risks of highly gendered policies like menstrual leave which, as discussed above, could have regressive outcomes for women at work by reinforcing gender stereotypes and increasing the cost of female labour. Evidence from some countries where menstrual leave is formally legislated, such as Indonesia and Japan, shows this benefit may be withheld or used to justify gender discrimination due to the costs (Baird, Hill & Colussi 2021). However, it is worth noting that concerns about cost and employer backlash characterised debates around paid maternity leave in the 1970s, which is now widely agreed to be an essential work–care policy despite the risks and financial costs (see Chapter 3).

Even if reproductive policies have a positive impact on women and gender equality at work, it is possible that some initiatives could reinforce other inequalities around work and family formation. For example, employer-provided benefits for IVF or egg freezing may offer support to workers within a company but pose a broader society-wide risk of embedding race and class inequalities in access to fertility treatment, which is both time and cost prohibitive for most people (Stone 2020). There is also the risk that reproductive policy could be used to promote market-based principles rather than work–care reconciliation. If menstrual leave is grounded in the assumption that employers need to fix the "problem" of periods to ensure business productivity, this could reinforce the idea that there is an inherent conflict between menstruation and paid work (Baird, Hill & Colussi 2021: 222; Goldblatt & Steele 2019: 298). Similar issues arise for fertility benefits. Not only could these policies incentivise delayed child-bearing in a context of declining fertility, they could also strengthen the expectation that young people should behave like the "ideal" or unencumbered worker for as long as biologically possible. If fertility benefits are made available to workers, then other family-oriented policies such as parental leave, child care and flexible work (see Chapters 3–5) should also be available. This approach is preferable to one-off payments for fertility treatments because it normalises starting a family while also acknowledging that reproductive and family responsibilities are a lifelong commitment that extend beyond conception and childbirth (Aubrey 2021).

2.5 Potential avenues for change

With policies to cater for the reproductive body at work gaining national and international momentum, there is an opportunity to improve the current policy architecture for these issues. We consider three potential avenues for change: public policy, bargaining and employer policy. We evaluate these options separately, but these approaches may overlap in practice, and it may therefore be necessary to explore all three avenues to develop a policy framework that can help all people work and care for their reproductive bodies.

Public policy

Public policy and legislative reform can potentially deliver the most expansive benefits in this area. For example, widening the scope of personal or "sick" leave under the National Employment Standards and *Fair Work Act* to explicitly include menstruation, fertility treatments and menopause as legitimate grounds for leave could provide clarity and protection for workers who wish to take paid leave for these issues. However, this would not resolve the inherent problem of categorising these processes as illnesses and requiring workers to use their sick leave. Another option that has been explored by Australian legal scholars in the context of menstruation (Golding & Hvala 2021: 350) and fertility treatments (Hvala 2018: 932) is to include a separate provision for paid leave in the National Employment Standards and *Fair Work Act*. This approach means workers would no longer have to take "sick" leave, while also making a clear and prescriptive benefit available to all national system employees (Hvala 2018: 930). Similar reforms could be pursued for pregnancy loss, such as amending existing legislation (see Table 2.1) to make these benefits available at any gestation, explicitly including abortion as a ground for leave and expanding paid leave options. Public investment in reproductive health and subsidies is another way to support the reproductive wellbeing of workers. Given the expense and loss of income that can be required to care for the reproductive body, public policies like the affordable IVF initiative and expansion of menopause services in New South Wales can help equalise access to support and treatment. However, as of October 2022, New South Wales was the only state with these types of initiatives, signalling the need for similar levels of investment in other states and territories and at the national level. As discussed above, it has also been suggested that the simplest approach would be to legislate a larger number of personal or "life leave" days that can be used for any personal or care-related issues. This approach would avoid some of the concerns regarding privacy, discussed above.

Bargaining

While Australian trade unions have a "deep masculinist" tradition, they have also played an important role in advancing issues of special interest to women such as pay equity, parental leave and domestic violence leave (Pocock & Brown 2012: 28). Union membership is now highly feminised (Cooper 2012), and the union movement is an appropriate forum in which to pursue reproductive leave and to potentially "mainstream" these policies in enterprise agreements across Australia (Kirton 2021: 596). There is also emerging evidence from overseas that union advocacy in this area is shaping public policy agendas. For example, in Ireland the Irish National Teachers Organisation was instrumental in advancing a new Bill to provide up to 20 days paid leave for miscarriage and fertility treatment that was under review in 2022 (O'Halloran 2021). However, an enterprise bargaining approach will only offer support to employees in workplaces covered by the agreement.

Employer policy

Some Australian employers are emerging as leaders in reproductive policy innovation, reflecting a desire to support workers while also gaining the economic and reputational benefits of gender-inclusive workplace practices. These employers are also responding to shortcomings in Australian work, care and family policy. Spotify argued that "if the government's not moving the needle, then maybe it's the job of private companies to take the lead here" (Aubrey 2021). Pursuing reproductive leave at the employer level may provide an opportunity to develop targeted policies that are more responsive to the specific needs of people in different types of work, while also setting new labour market standards. However, as with bargaining, this approach will result in significant gaps in coverage. At this stage, only a small number of companies with progressive agendas are introducing these policies. As a result, relying on the private sector to deliver change may reinforce race and class inequalities in this area if there are no public policies that offer support for these issues.

2.6 Conclusion

Workplace policies for the reproductive body are an important addition to the work, care and family policy architecture in Australia, but as yet there is no clear or correct path forward. However, it is important to recognise the unique historical moment. With the COVID-19 pandemic disrupting traditional approaches to work and policymakers advocating for a gender-equal recovery, there is an opportunity to reimagine the social contract and its assumptions and expectations of workers, including notions of an ideal or disembodied worker. If governments and employers can accept the reproductive wellbeing of all people as a public "good" rather than a workplace disruption, this may have transformative implications for the structure of work and help Australia have a more age and gender diverse workforce.

References

Ahwan, L. (2022). More companies offering fertility benefits to workers. *Daily Telegraph,* 21 March. https://bit.ly/3NhUw2i.

AMWU promotes menstrual leave. *Sydney Morning Herald* online, 11 February 2005. https://bit.ly/3GAxaBc.

Ashurst (2021). Ashurst launches landmark global parental leave policy – strengthens supports for working parents. Web page, 28 July. https://bit.ly/489pWQ8.

Atkins, C. (2020). For transgender men, pain of menstruation is more than just physical. *NBC News,* 12 January. https://bit.ly/3uGZ8bx.

Atkinson, C., Carmichael, F. and Duberley, J. (2021). The menopause taboo at work: examining women's embodied experiences of menopause in the UK police service. *Work, Employment and Society* 35(4), 657–676. https://doi.org/10.1177/0950017020971573.

Aubrey, S. (2021). IVF on us: Spotify leads the way with family benefits for Australian staff. *Sydney Morning Herald,* 10 October. https://bit.ly/3F6sRNf.

Australian Bureau of Statistics (2021a). Australian fertility rate hits record low. Media release, 8 December. https://bit.ly/3GA4PL4.

Australian Bureau of Statistics (2021b). *Births, Australia.* Canberra: Australian Bureau of Statistics. https://bit.ly/3t79XTS.

Australian Human Rights Commission (2014). *Supporting Working Parents: Pregnancy and Return to Work National Review.* https://bit.ly/3RgBs5s.

Australian Nursing and Midwifery Federation (2020). Paid leave for IVF treatment sets new precedent. 18 November. https://bit.ly/3tbMsJp.

Baird, M, Hill, E and Colussi, S (2022). What can unions do for the reproductive body at work? [Manuscript in preparation]. Discipline of Work and Organisational Studies, University of Sydney.

Baird, M., Hill, E. and Colussi, S. (2021). Mapping menstrual leave legislation and policy historically and globally: a labor entitlement to reinforce, remedy or revolutionise gender equality at work. *Comparative Labor Law and Policy Journal* 42(1): 187–225.

Baird, M., Hamilton, M., Dinale, D., Gulesserian, L. and Heron, A. (2022). Broadening our conception of leave: leave to care for self or others over the life course. In I. Dobrotić, S. Blum and A. Koslowski, eds. *Research Handbook on Leave Policy: Parenting and Social Inequalities in a Global Perspective*, 368–83. Cheltenham: Edward Elgar Publishing. https://doi.org/10.4337/9781800372214.

Balogh, S. (2005). Union calls grow for menstrual leave. *Courier Mail,* 12 February.

Barrington, D.J., Robinson, H.J., Wilson, E. and Hennegan, J. (2021). Experiences of menstruation in high income countries: a systematic review, qualitative evidence synthesis and comparison to low- and middle-income countries. *PLoS ONE* 16(7): 1–44.

BBC News (2021). Menstrual leave: South Korea Airline ex-CEO fined for refusing time off. *BBC News* online, 25 April. https://bit.ly/46OD2Bh.

Beck, V., Brewis, J. and Davies, A. (2021). Women's experiences of menopause at work and performance management. *Organization* 28(3): 510–20.

Bell, J. (2021). Future Super introduces menstrual and menopause leave. *Human Resources Director,* 15 April. https://bit.ly/48pdfkj.

Brewis, J., Beck, V., Davies, A. and Matheson, J. (2017). *The Effects of Menopause Transition on Women's Economic Participation in the UK.* London: Department for Education.

British Medical Association (2020). *Challenging the Culture on Menopause for Working Doctors.* https://bit.ly/3Fau85K.

Bucci, N. and Willingham, R. (2015). Victorian police accept lower 2.5 per cent annual pay rise but gain weekend penalty rates. *Age,* 10 December. https://bit.ly/3ZMoQH2.

Commonwealth Bank of Australia (2020). CBA increases parental leave support for employees. 24 August. https://bit.ly/4a8v4G6.

Cooper, R. (2012). The gender gap in union leadership in Australia: a qualitative study. *Journal of Industrial Relations* 54(2): 131–46.

Colussi, S., Hill, E. and Baird, M. (2022). We're putting gender at the heart of the Fair Work Act, but there's still no compassionate leave for abortions. *The Conversation*, 10 November. https://bit.ly/3tjBCka.

Cormack, L. (2022). $40.3m funding boost to support women facing 'debilitating' reality of menopause. *Sydney Morning Herald*, 10 June. https://bit.ly/473pthD.

Denholm, M. (2003). Female uni staff fight for monthly stress leave. *Daily Telegraph*, 28 February.

Fair Work Commission (2022). What is a national system employer? https://www.fwc.gov.au/what-national-system-employer.

Fair Work Ombudsman (2022a). Compassionate and bereavement leave. https://www.fairwork.gov.au/leave/compassionate-and-bereavement-leave.

Fair Work Ombudsman (2022b). Parental leave for stillbirth, premature birth or infant death. https://bit.ly/3RyhK6z.

Fair Work Ombudsman (2022c). Pregnant employee entitlements. https://bit.ly/3Nj3xrT.

Filmer, H. (2022). Auckland woman takes her manager to human rights tribunal over period stigma. *Re News*, 26 February. https://bit.ly/48JhmJ7.

Foley, M. and Cooper, R. (2021). Workplace gender equality in the post-pandemic era: where to next? *Journal of Industrial Relations* 63(4): 463–76.

Francis, A. (2022). Could "menstrual leave" change the workplace? *BBC News* online, 29 April. https://bit.ly/3NjCHjj.

Goldblatt, G. and Steele, L. (2019). Bloody unfair: Inequality related to menstruation – considering the role of discrimination law. *Sydney Law Review* 41(3): 293–326.

Golding, G. (2021). Major court and tribunal decisions in Australia in 2020. *Journal of Industrial Relations* 63(3): 395–410.

Golding, G. and Hvala, T. (2021). Paid period leave for Australian women: a prerogative not a pain. *Sydney Law Review* 43(3): 349–77.

Grandey, A.A., Gabriel, A.S. and King, E.B. (2020). Tackling taboo topics: a review of the three Ms in working women's lives. *Journal of Management* 46(1): 7–35.

Health and Community Services Union (2020). Why HACSU is fighting for reproductive health and wellbeing leave. Web page, 18 September. https://bit.ly/3thk7Bn.

Hill, A. (2021). Menopause at centre of increasing number of UK employment tribunals. *Guardian*, 7 August. https://bit.ly/3RwNIQB.

Hill, E., Baird, M., Vromen, A., Cooper, R., Meers, Z. and Probyn, E. (2019). Young women and men: imagined futures of work and family formation in Australia. *Journal of Sociology* 55(4): 778–98.

Hislop, M. (2021). NSW government to introduce paid miscarriage and stillbirth leave in public sector. *Women's Agenda*, 22 June. https://bit.ly/3rPAQLl.

HR Daily (2022). Life leave gives employees privacy and autonomy. Web page. https://bit.ly/3Njxnw6.

Hvala, T. (2018). In vital need of reform: providing certainty for working women undergoing IVF treatment. *UNSW Law Journal* 41(3): 901–38.

Karin, M.L. (2022). Addressing periods at work. *Harvard Law and Policy Review* 16.

King, S. (2021). Menstrual leave: good intention, poor solution. In J. Hassard and L.D. Torres, eds. *Aligning Perspectives in Gender Mainstreaming: Aligning Perspectives on Health, Safety and Well-Being*, 151–76. Cham, Switzerland: Springer Nature.

Kirton, G. (2021). Union framing of gender equality and the elusive potential of equality bargaining in a difficult climate. *Journal of Industrial Relations* 63(4): 591–613.

Markey, R. and McIvor, J. (2018). Regulating casual employment in Australia. *Journal of Industrial Relations* 60(5): 593–618.

McCarthy, M., Molan, J., Gichuhi, L., Keneally, K. and Rice, J. (2018). *Select Committee on Stillbirth Research and Education*. Senate Report: Parliament House, Canberra. https://bit.ly/46J6N6J.

Melican, C. and Mountford, G. (2017). Why we've introduced a menstrual policy and you should too. Victorian Women's Trust, Blog post, 23 May. https://www.vwt.org.au/blog-menstrual-policy/.

Meunier, S., de Montigny, F., Zeghiche, S., Lalande, D., Verdon, C., Da Costa, D. and Feeley, N. (2021). Workplace experience of parents coping with perinatal loss: A scoping review. *Work* 69(2): 411–21. https://doi.org/10.3233/WOR-213487.

Muldowney, S. (2021). Why it's time to talk about menopause at work. *In the Black*, 1 October. https://bit.ly/419TPh7.

Munro, A.K. (2022). *Periods Impact Potential: Findings from the Australian Department of Health 2021 Menstrual Health Survey Report*. Canberra: Australian Government Department of Health.

Muroi, M. (2022). Could Australia follow Spain by introducing national menstrual leave? *Sydney Morning Herald*, 21 May. https://bit.ly/3ZMT2Su.

Nelson, S (2021). Modibodi launches menstrual, menopause & miscarriage paid leave. Modibodi, Blog post, 4 May. https://bit.ly/3RHWdIZ.

New South Wales Health (2022). Improving affordability and access to IVF services in NSW. Web page, 30 May. https://bit.ly/3uXoX7h.

Newman, J.E., Paul, R.C. and Chambers, G.M. (2021). *Assisted Reproductive Technology in Australia and New Zealand 2019*. Report. Sydney: National Perinatal Epidemiology and Statistics Unit, the University of New South Wales. https://bit.ly/3RwNJUD.

Obst, K.L., Due, C., Oxlad, M. and Middleton, P. (2020). Australian men's experiences of leave provisions and workplace supporting following pregnancy loss or neonatal death. *Community, Work and Family* 25(4): 551–62.

O'Halloran, M. (2021). Bill aims to provide paid leave for early miscarriage. *Irish Times*, 24 May. https://bit.ly/3NjYNCe.

Pocock, B. and Brown, K. (2012). Gendered leadership in Australian unions in the process of strategic renewal: instrumental, transformative or post-heroic? In S. Ledwith and L.L. Hansen, eds. *Gendering and Diversifying Trade Union Leadership*, 27–46. New York: Routledge.

Porschitz, E.T. and Siler, E.A. (2017). Miscarriage in the workplace: an autoethnography. *Gender, Work and Organization* 24(6): 565–78.

Prasser, K. (2021). A bloody good policy. *Future Super*, 12 February. https://www.futuresuper.com.au/blog/a-bloody-good-policy/.

Pryor, L. and AAP. (2005). Female workers ask for paid menstrual leave. *Sydney Morning Herald* online, 11 February. https://bit.ly/3TxyQDh.

Queensland Teachers' Union (2020). The QTU Menopause Project. *Queensland Teachers' Journal* online, 6 November. https://bit.ly/3uW0uiF.

Read, M. (2022). Government pledges $139m for endometriosis support and genetic testing. *Australian Financial Review*, 24 March. https://bit.ly/3Q8TtDp.

Robertson, D. (2017). Memories of Hoddle St: 30 years on. *The Police Association Victoria Journal* 84(4): 1–58.

Rose, A. and Oxlad, M. (2022). LGBTQ+ peoples' experiences of workplace leave and support following pregnancy loss. *Community, Work and Family* 26(2): 268–84.

Schoep, M., Adang, E., Maas, J., De Bie, B., Aarts, J. and Neiboer, T. (2019). Productivity loss due to menstruation-related symptoms: a nationwide cross-sectional survey among 32,748 women. *BMJ Open* 9(6): 1–10.

Shams, H. (2021). Menstrual leave adopted by more Australian businesses as debate grows around policy. *ABC News*, 24 June.https://bit.ly/4a9JHJ8.

Silva, A. (2022). ANZ introduces paid gender affirmation leave. What is it and what other types of leave are there? *ABC News*, 7 June. https://bit.ly/3TgE85N.

Stone, A. (2020). More and more companies are covering the cost of egg freezing. but who is it really for? *Vice*, 26 May. https://bit.ly/3LPckAU.

Tuohy, W. (2020). Reproductive leave claim an Australian first. *Age*, 13 September. https://bit.ly/3Mgimej.

Unions seek "menstrual leave" for Toyota workers. *ABC News* online, 11 February 2005. https://bit.ly/47MCZHA.

Victorian Women's Trust (2021). Menstrual and menopause workplace wellbeing policy. https://bit.ly/41gTf1c.

Walker, K. (2003). A time to leave: no questions asked. *Courier-Mail*, 7 March.

Whittard, J. (2021). Gender affirmation leave: bargaining for better workplaces, better UON! *National Tertiary Education Union* online, 28 October. https://bit.ly/3tdqmX5.

Young, K., Fisher, J. and Kirkman, M. (2015). Women's experiences of endometriosis: a systematic review and synthesis of qualitative research. *Journal of Family Planning and Reproductive Health Care* 41: 225–34.

Zip Co (2021). Miscarriage bereavement policy. Web page, 28 April. https://bit.ly/3uRxCbC.

3
Parental leave policy: Time to grow

Marian Baird and Gillian Whitehouse

3.1 Introduction

Parental leave is a cornerstone of work and family policy that helps new parents combine paid work with their family roles and responsibilities. Ideally, in addition to the promise of health and economic benefits, such policies should enhance women's economic opportunities and gender equality in the domestic division of work and care. However, as research has long shown, such outcomes are far from guaranteed (see OECD 2012: 171–2; Ruhm 1998).

Overwhelmingly, it is women as mothers who take leave from work to care for babies, setting in train a series of other labour market-related inequalities relative to men, including lower rates of labour force participation, shorter hours of work on return from parenting-related leave, lower pay reflected in a motherhood pay gap, reduced access to training and career advancement, and lower superannuation accumulations (Baird & Heron 2020). However, well-designed parental leave has the potential to challenge social norms and related gender inequalities and to deliver significant social and economic benefits, especially where it normalises usage by both parents and provides pathways for men and fathers to participate in child care.

In this chapter, we assess the capacity of Australian parental leave policies to assist new parents and incentivise shared opportunities for work and care. Our primary focus is on provisions at the national level, where unpaid *maternity* leave was adopted in 1979, and extended to unpaid *parental* leave in 1990, but not complemented with *paid parental leave* until 2010. National paid parental leave provisions have been amended only slightly since their inception and it is their strengths and limitations, along with possibilities for advancement, that form the central thread of our analysis. Other (employer-provided) parental leave provisions, including the entitlements that federal, state and territory governments provide for public sector employees and those offered by many private and non-government sector employers are also addressed, albeit in less detail.

The chapter begins with an overview of the Australian policy architecture, explaining the combination of public policy with the role of employers (in the public and private sectors) in providing paid parental leave, and noting the terminology that has been adopted for the various provisions. We provide a detailed overview of the development and scope of statutory provisions at the national level, as these are the standards to which the majority of Australians have access, and which have received the most policy attention in the last decade. This is followed by a synopsis of employer-provided entitlements. We then turn to current debates, raising several critical issues and points of unresolved tension in this policy area, including leave duration and pay levels, the lack of superannuation in the national statutory paid leave scheme, gaps in access depending on women's labour market position and the highly gendered patterns of uptake. In conclusion, we consider potential avenues for positive change, including increasing the duration of parental leave and enabling a more equitable uptake by mothers and fathers.

3.2 Current Australian policy architecture and terminology

The policy architecture of parental leave in Australia is complex, involving not only national statutory entitlements for paid and unpaid leave legislated by the federal government, but also the schemes provided by federal, state and territory governments for their public sector employees and those of private and non-government sector employers. These components are set out in Table 3.1, which presents policy information by provider.

To further complicate matters, the terminology adopted varies considerably across these different policy strands and jurisdictions, as well as differing from international usage. While there is some variation in how parental leave policies are defined and designed from country to country, a common pattern is a combination of "maternity", "paternity" and "parental" leave. In this combination, "maternity" and "paternity" refer to separate leave entitlements available immediately following the birth or adoption of a child for the mother and father respectively, while "parental leave" refers to a shared family leave entitlement following maternity or paternity leave, to enable parents to care for an infant over an extended period (Dobrotić & Blum 2020: 589). However, not only are the distinctions between these leave types increasingly blurred (Koslowski et al. 2021: 3), Australia is also idiosyncratic in its frequent and longstanding use of "parental leave" as an overarching term covering maternity, paternity and parental leaves.

These complexities are illustrated in Table 3.1, which provides details on the range of parental leave policies and the labels applied to them in the different Australian jurisdictions. The first panel provides information on the statutory entitlements provided at the national level. These include unpaid parental leave, provided by the *Fair Work Act 2009* (Cth) and accessible to all employees under the national industrial relations system (which covers most Australian employees) who meet the eligibility criteria; Parental Leave Pay (PLP), provided by the *Paid Parental Leave Act 2010* (Cth) and accessible to all Australian employees and self-employed workers who meet the eligibility criteria; and Dad and Partner Pay (DaPP), also provided by the *Paid Parental Leave Act* and thus with the same accessibility as parental leave pay. The unpaid leave and parental leave pay provisions use the generic term "parental" to indicate that they are – in principle – accessible by either parent, while Dad and Partner Pay sets aside a protected period of leave for fathers or partners.

The second panel in Table 3.1 refers to the provisions made available for public sector employees by federal, state and territory governments in their role as employers. There is a great deal of variation in terminology across jurisdictions, with terms such as "maternity" and "spousal" leave frequently used in legislative and regulatory provisions. For example, the Queensland Paid Parental Leave Directive refers to maternity, adoption, surrogacy, long spousal, short spousal, pre-natal, pre-adoption and pre-surrogacy leave (Queensland Government 2020).

The final panel of Table 3.1 refers to private or non-government sector entitlements provided by employer policies or enterprise agreements. Among these policies, terms such as "primary" and "secondary" carer leave have been more commonly adopted, but, as discussed below, there is a move to abandon this distinction.

3.3 The development and use of national statutory parental leave policies in Australia

The history of parental leave at the national level and its development in legislation have produced a framework of statutory measures defined by a mix of industrial and welfare policies (Whitehouse & Brady 2019; Brennan 2009; Baird 2005). In 1912, a welfare payment known as a "maternity allowance" was one of the first policies made available to new mothers, but the concept of "parental leave" emerged much later as an industrial rather than social security entitlement. This has led to the construction of a hybrid system in which both unpaid and paid entitlements are now employment-based (contingent on employment status and participation in paid work), while payments are funded through general revenue and managed through social policy machinery. The historical development and use of these policies are outlined below.

The provision of unpaid maternity and parental leave

In 1978, the Australian Council of Trade Unions (ACTU), under the leadership of Secretary Bob Hawke, brought the first test case of its kind for unpaid maternity leave and the right to job protection for working women to the federal Industrial Relations Commission. The task of

Table 3.1 Parental leave policies in Australia by provider, 2022

Provision	Recipient	Duration (a)	Payment	Eligibility criteria (b)
1: National statutory entitlements (enacted by the federal government)				
Unpaid Parental Leave (*Fair Work Act*)	Each parent	12 months	Unpaid	12 months employment (c)
Parental Leave Pay (*Paid Parental Leave Act*)	Primary carer (birth or adoptive mother in first instance)	18 weeks	National Minimum Wage	Work, income and residency tests
Dad and Partner Pay (DaPP) (*Paid Parental Leave Act*)	Father, or mother's partner	2 weeks	National Minimum Wage	Work, income and residency tests
2a: Federal government entitlements for public sector employees				
Maternity Leave (*Maternity Leave (Cth Employees) Act*)	Mothers	12 weeks	Replacement wage	12 months employment
2b: State and territory government entitlements for public sector employees				
Parental leave (variously labelled)	Primary carer Secondary carer	14 weeks 1 week	Replacement wage	12 months employment
3: Private/non-government sector employer-provided entitlements				
Parental leave (variously labelled)	Primary carer Secondary carer	11 weeks 1–2 weeks	Replacement wage	12 months employment

Notes: (a) As specified in the Acts cited, or as an average where provisions vary (as in Panels 2b and 3); (b) As specified in the Acts cited, or the most common requirement where criteria vary (as in Panels 2b and 3); (c) Also available to 'regular' casual employees, i.e. those who have been employed as a casual during a period of at least 12 months prior to the birth or adoption and would have a reasonable expectation of continuing employment (*Fair Work Act*, s 67(2)).

Sources: Panel 1 – *Fair Work Act*, *Paid Parental Leave Act*; Panel 2a – *Maternity Leave (Commonwealth Employees) Act 1973*; Panel 2b – various state/territory Acts, government directives and enterprise agreements; Panel 3 – based on data from Workplace Gender Equality Agency 2020–21 survey of non-public sector organisations with 100 or more employees (Workplace Gender Equality Agency 2022: 25).

running the case was given to the newly appointed Jan Marsh, who was also the ACTU's first female industrial officer. In 1979, the Industrial Relations Commission awarded 52 weeks or 12 months unpaid maternity leave to women workers, arguing that working conditions should reflect the rapid increase in women's workforce participation (Baird 2005). The decision also conferred the right to job protection, enabling women to return to their pre-maternity leave position or, if it was no longer available, to one that was nearest in status and pay. In 1985, the commission extended the right to 12 months unpaid leave to adoptive parents and in 1990, following another ACTU claim, the commission further extended the entitlement to fathers and renamed the provision "parental leave" (Baird 2005).

The term "parental leave" was retained when the entitlement was first incorporated into federal industrial relations legislation in 1993. With the passage of the *Fair Work Act 2009* (Cth), unpaid parental leave became one of the 10 National Employment Standards. At the same time, the 12 months leave entitlement was extended to 12 months *per parent* (rather than per couple), with the right to request an extension of up to 24 months for one employed parent if the other did not use their portion. However, employers may refuse this request on "reasonable business grounds" if the request does not meet the operational needs of the business. All employees, including casuals, with 12 months continuous experience now have access to 52 weeks unpaid parental leave. The requirement for 12 months continuous employment may be waived if an enterprise agreement has different eligibility criteria.

All unpaid parental leave must be taken within 24 months of the child's birth or adoption. For the mother, the leave can start from the date of birth or adoption, or from up to six weeks before the expected date of birth or earlier if the employer agrees. When both members of a couple are entitled to unpaid parental leave, they can take eight weeks of this leave at the same time. This leave must be taken within 12 months of birth or adoption.

Some flexibilities have been incorporated into unpaid parental leave in recent years. Following amendments to the *Fair Work Act* in

2020,[1] up to 30 days (six weeks) of "flexible unpaid parental leave" can be taken by either parent within the first 24 months following birth or adoption, either as a single continuous period or as separate periods of one or more days. While providing more flexibility than the single block of leave previously allowed, the total amount of unpaid parental leave per parent, in the absence of an extension as outlined above, remains one year.

Use of unpaid parental leave

Due to lack of comprehensive data collection, the use of unpaid parental leave benefits is difficult to estimate. However, available data from the Australian Bureau of Statistics Pregnancy and Employment Transitions Survey in 2017 indicated that, among women with a child under two years of age who worked as an employee while pregnant and did not permanently leave their job before the birth of their child, 65 per cent had taken unpaid leave, with a median duration of 18 weeks (Australian Bureau of Statistics 2017: Table 7.1; see also Whitehouse, Baird & Baxter 2021).[2] These figures suggest widespread use of the unpaid parental leave benefit, although for shorter periods than the full entitlement, with the median duration coinciding with the duration of the national statutory paid leave entitlement.

The same survey indicated that, among women with a child under two years of age who had a partner who worked as an employee during her pregnancy, unpaid leave usage was considerably lower for their partners. Only around 16 per cent of partners (assumed in the main to be fathers) took unpaid leave, with a median duration of two weeks (Australian Bureau of Statistics 2017: Table 22.1). However, almost two-thirds of partners took some paid leave, also for a median duration of two weeks (Australian Bureau of Statistics 2017: Table 22.1). This is consistent with previous research, which has found that fathers tend to take paid annual leave (or other forms of accrued paid leave) at or around the birth or adoption of a child (Whitehouse et al. 2006).

---

1   *Fair Work Amendment (Improving Unpaid Parental Leave for Parents of Stillborn Babies and Other Measures) Act 2020* (Cth).
2   The most recent survey at the time of writing.

The introduction of Australia's Paid Parental Leave scheme

Compared with other countries, many of which had introduced paid maternity leave benefits by the early 1970s, Australia was late in developing a paid parental leave scheme. While a scheme had been argued for on numerous occasions over the 20th century, pressures to introduce a national paid parental leave scheme did not come to a head until 2000. At this point, declining fertility rates, increasing female workforce participation rates, increasing attention to work– family tensions and Australia's poor international standing on these issues set the context for policy activism and government reaction. In this context, the Human Rights and Equal Opportunity Commission (now called the Australian Human Rights Commission) published important reports in the early 2000s, calling for 14 weeks paid maternity leave, in line with the ILO Maternity Protection Convention 2000 (No. 183) (Human Rights and Equal Opportunity Commission 2002a, 2002b).

However, the first significant policy response, from the federal Howard (Coalition) government in 2004, came in the form of a maternity cash payment rather than a comprehensive parental leave policy. The federal government passed the *Family Assistance Legislation Amendment (More Help for Families – Increased Payments) Act 2004* (Cth) to provide a "Maternity Payment" – later dubbed the "Baby Bonus". Motivated primarily by pronatalist concerns about falling fertility rates (Baird & Cutcher 2005), the government provided a cash payment for each baby, regardless of the mother's workforce status or income. It was eventually removed in 2014, replaced with a smaller loading on the family tax benefit (see Chapter 7 on tax and transfer policies in this volume), targeting the payment more directly to lower income families (Kladpor 2013–14).

The union movement, women's groups and some business groups continued to lobby the federal government for a paid parental leave scheme, but it was not until a Labor government was elected federally in 2007 that the "economic case", based on the importance of enabling higher female labour force participation rates, was promoted and accepted as a key rationale for the *Paid Parental Leave Act 2010* (Cth). The other objectives of the new scheme were maternal and child health and gender equality (Productivity Commission 2009).

In 2010, the Labor government introduced Australia's first paid parental leave scheme, which commenced operation from January 2011. While the *Fair Work Act* provides the right to unpaid parental *leave* from work, as discussed above, it is the *Paid Parental Leave Act* that provides the right to *payment*, which is referred to as Parental Leave Pay (PLP).

The *Paid Parental Leave Act* provides 18 weeks pay at the National Minimum Wage[3] to the primary carer, assumed to be the birth or adoptive mother, who under certain circumstances can transfer the payment to another primary carer. It is subject to certain eligibility criteria including residency, work and income requirements. Recipients can be self-employed or employees, in permanent or casual employment, but must be Australian residents and have completed 330 hours of work over a 10-month period within the 13 months prior to birth or adoption (equivalent to approximately one day per week in the 10 months prior to birth or adoption), with no more than a 12-week gap between workdays. The income test is set at the mother's income, with a cap in 2020–21 of AU$151,350 adjusted taxable income earned in the previous financial year.

In contrast to most other countries, Australia does not have a national insurance system where workers and employers contribute to a fund covering welfare payments such as unemployment benefits and parental leave. This means funding for the Paid Parental Leave scheme relies on general taxation revenue, which was one of the reasons for the delay in introducing a national paid scheme and remains a barrier to further expanding the scheme (Whitehouse, Baird & Morrissey 2022). Another distinctive element of the scheme, designed to encourage an ongoing connection between employees and employers, is that the default position is for the payment to be made via the employer payroll system to the employee while they are on parental leave. In 2019–20, almost 70 per cent of Parental Leave Pay recipients were paid via their employer (Department of Social Services 2021).[4]

---

3   The National Minimum Wage is set and reviewed annually by an Expert Panel of the Fair Work Commission.
4   This is the most recent available data as it was not provided in the Department of Social Services annual report for 2020–21.

The original scheme did not explicitly provide paid leave for fathers. This was addressed in 2012 when the *Paid Parental Leave Act* was amended to provide "Dad and Partner Pay" (DaPP),[5] a two-week entitlement paid at the National Minimum Wage, exclusively for fathers or same-sex partners. This payment is not transferrable to the mother.

Since 2013, the Paid Parental Leave scheme (referring to both PLP and DaPP) has attracted considerable political attention. In early 2014, new conservative Prime Minister Tony Abbott proposed a more generous Paid Parental Leave scheme for working mothers, with a plan to fund the proposal via a levy on big business (Whitehouse & Brady 2019). Referred to as his "signature policy", the scheme aimed to provide 26 weeks pay at income replacement levels for mothers earning up to $150,000 per annum, or a maximum of $75,000 (Abbott 2009). This was later reduced to an income cap of $100,000 per annum, or a maximum of $50,000 parental leave pay. While the Abbott proposal was longer and more generous for mothers, it was less gender equitable as there was no specific leave for fathers or partners (Baird & O'Brien 2015). The proposal was resisted by business, widely criticised as being too expensive and providing middle-class welfare and was dropped by the federal government in early 2015 (Grattan 2015).

The next proposal for change came in 2015 when then Treasurer Joe Hockey announced, somewhat ironically on Mother's Day, the federal government planned to reduce the overall period of government-funded leave available to mothers by deducting any period of employer-provided paid parental leave from the total 18 weeks provided by the government scheme. This was widely opposed and mothers around Australia were insulted by the accusation they were "double-dipping" and "rorting" the system when they were using it exactly as it had been designed (Work + Family Policy Roundtable 2015). An attempt to amend the legislation was made in 2016, but this proposal too was widely opposed and eventually lapsed. Since then, the Paid Parental Leave scheme has remained largely unchanged with only minor adjustments allowing for greater flexibility of use and a widened work test, introduced in 2021.

---

5   Paid Parental Leave and Other Legislation Amendment (Dad and Partner Pay and Other Measures) Bill 2012.

In early 2022, just prior to the federal election due by May, the Coalition government, led by Prime Minister Scott Morrison, outlined a new proposal that combined the 18 weeks paid leave for the "primary" carer and two weeks for Dads and Partners into a single 20-week entitlement to be accessed by either parent, at any time within the two years following birth or adoption. Sole parents would also receive 20 weeks, rather than 18 weeks. Under this proposal, however, there was no longer a separate period of paid leave reserved for fathers, raising concerns that it no longer incentivised fathers to take on active caring roles as new parents. A second change related to the income test, with a proposal to change the eligibility cap based solely on the mother's income to a household cap of $350,000 per annum. The changes announced also did not include payment of superannuation to new parents during parental leave, a proposal that had been recommended in a Treasury review of retirement income in 2020 (Australian Government Treasury 2020). Following the election of the Albanese Labor government in May 2022, these proposals were overtaken by the new government's agenda and significant changes to paid parental are in train, as we discuss below.

Use of the Paid Parental Leave scheme

In designing the scheme that became operative in 2011, one of the main aims of the Labor government and the Social Services Minister Jenny Macklin was to ensure that lower paid women, who typically have no access to employer provisions, received some form of paid parental leave. Prior to its introduction, only around half of the employed female workforce had access to employer-provided paid maternity leave (Martin et al. 2012: 19). A government-commissioned review of the new national scheme found that it enabled mothers to extend their leave from work by up to six months and that this effect was "most pronounced amongst mothers on lower incomes and with lower formal education, including those who had been on casual contracts before the birth of their baby" (Martin et al. 2014: 5). A later study found that the scheme had "a positive impact on mothers taking leave in the first half year and on mothers' probability of returning to work in the first year" and also found "that disadvantaged mothers – low income, less educated, [and] without access to employer-funded leave" responded most to the new benefits (Broadway et al. 2020: 30).

In the first full year of operation, around 44 per cent of new mothers received some parental leave pay (Department of Families, Housing, Community Services and Indigenous Affairs 2012: 50), increasing to around 51 per cent in 2019 (Department of Social Services 2020: 76).[6] The proportion of mothers taking the full 18 weeks has remained consistently high since the scheme commenced, and in 2020 just over 99 per cent of recipients took the full 18 weeks (Department of Social Services 2021: 98–9). It is estimated that only around 27 per cent of men who became fathers in the 2019–20 financial year took some DaPP (Whitehouse, Baird & Baxter 2021). However, among fathers and partners who took DaPP in that year, 97 per cent claimed the full two weeks benefit (Department of Social Services 2020: 76).

In summary, both the statutory unpaid and paid parental leave provisions are used predominately by women, and the specific paid entitlement for fathers and partners, DaPP, is not widely used by men. The result is that, while a major gap in the work–family policy landscape was filled when the Paid Parental Leave scheme was first introduced in 2011, the overall policy framework remains modest and does not challenge the highly gendered division of care responsibilities between women and men in Australia.

3.4 Employer-provided paid parental leave

The second important component of Australia's parental leave policy architecture is employer-provided paid parental leave. Under the national statutory scheme, employers can top-up the payment (at the National Minimum Wage) to regular wage levels for the 18 weeks, but Workplace Gender Equality Agency figures indicate that only 10 per cent of non-public sector organisations with 100 or more employees were doing so in 2021 (Workplace Gender Equality Agency Data Explorer) and it is more common for employers to provide their own

---

6   Note that not all new mothers are working at the time of birth.

separate schemes. These additional employer-provided paid leave policies can be categorised under two groups: those provided by federal, state and territory governments to public sector workers in each jurisdiction; and those provided by private and non-government sector employers (see Table 3.1).

Public sector employer-paid parental leave

The federal government and each of the states and territories have paid parental leave schemes for their own public sector workers, either as a legislated entitlement or government regulation or through an enterprise agreement. Table 3.2 shows that the duration of leave for the birth parent ranges from 12 to 18 weeks and that governments in all states and territories provide paternity or "secondary" carer leave, ranging from one day to 14 weeks. The federal government differs: the national legislation,[7] introduced in 1973, was the first to provide paid maternity leave, and is under review in 2022, with many submissions expected to recommend the extension of paid parental leave to fathers or partners.

In October 2022, the NSW government removed the distinction between "primary" and "secondary" carers in its policy, providing 14 weeks paid leave for each parent working in the public sector and two weeks additional paid leave if both parents take their portion of leave. This design is a first for Australian public sector policy and reflects a more Scandinavian approach, providing equal portions to mothers and fathers plus an incentive for both to use the leave. Additionally, in 2022, the NSW government introduced stillbirth and miscarriage leave as well as five days paid fertility treatment leave for its public sector employees (see Chapter 2 in this volume). These policies are also gaining greater attention in the private sector and in time may influence other state and territory governments to amend their schemes.

---

7   *The Maternity Leave (Commonwealth Employees) Act 1973 (Cth).*

Table 3.2 Duration of federal, state and territory public sector parental, maternity and paternity leave policies, (a) 2022

Jurisdiction	Duration (weeks) for the birth parent	Duration (weeks) for the other parent
Federal	12	0
New South Wales	14	14 (b)
Victoria	14	2
Queensland	14	1
South Australia	14	2
Western Australia	14	2
Tasmania	12	0.2 (1 day)
Australian Capital Territory	18	2
Northern Territory	14 (1–5 years service) 18 (> 5 years service)	1 (1–5 years service) 2 (> 5 years service)

Notes: (a) Terminology varies across jurisdictions with multiple labels in use, including parental leave, primary carer leave, secondary carer leave, other parent leave, spousal leave, adoption leave, surrogacy leave and bonding leave; (b) Plus an additional two weeks if both parents use the leave.

Private and non-government sector employer-paid parental leave

Not all private sector employers in Australia provide paid parental leave, but the proportion of those that do has been growing slightly each year, particularly among larger companies (Workplace Gender Equality Agency 2022). These provisions may be introduced unilaterally by companies or as a result of union–employer bargaining (Baird, Hamilton & Constantin 2021). In 2021, 60 per cent of Australian private sector employers (with 100 or more employees) provided employer-funded paid parental leave, with an average duration of 11 weeks (Workplace Gender Equality Agency 2022). Among the companies offering employer-funded paid parental leave, 100 per cent provide the same benefit to adoptive parents, 64 per cent cover stillbirth and 60 per cent cover surrogacy (Workplace Gender Equality Agency 2022). Almost three-quarters of employers now also provide superannuation on their own schemes, and 70 per cent pay superannuation on the government scheme. However, 19 per cent pay no superannuation on parental leave at all (Workplace Gender Equality Agency 2022).

Over half (55 per cent) of private sector employers providing paid parental leave extend this benefit to both women and men, reflecting a growing trend to "de-gender" the terminology and the entitlement and to remove the distinction between "primary" carer leave (assumed for mothers) and "secondary" carer leave (assumed for fathers). Despite this trend, women are still more likely than men to take the leave, with available data showing only 12 per cent of those taking employer-provided parental leave are men (Workplace Gender Equality Agency 2022).

3.5 Current tensions and debates

Debate over the design and implementation of paid parental leave under both the government and employer-provided schemes is ongoing in Australia (Baird et al. 2021; Wood, Emslie & Griffiths 2021). Key issues include duration and gender-equal access, level of pay, superannuation and the role of the private sector in providing paid parental leave.

Duration and gender-equal access

Australia's current national statutory scheme is criticised for its relatively short duration and lack of incentives for fathers to "share the care". For mothers, advocates argue that a longer period of leave between at least 26 weeks and one year is needed, and that this longer period should be available over the first two years of a child's life. The argument for longer paid parental leave is linked to research evidence on maternal and child health and breastfeeding (Lauzon-Guillain et al. 2019; Van Niel et al. 2019; Mirkovic, Perrine & Scanlon 2016; Cooklin, Rowe & Fisher 2012). Lack of access to early childhood education and care for very young children and parental preferences about familial care of infants are also given as reasons for longer paid leave (see Chapter 4). A longer period would also align with the OECD average of around 51 weeks (OECD Family Database 2022). The gendered design and the low rates of uptake by fathers and partners are other major causes for concern. To address this issue, policy advocates argue for a separate component of at least six weeks paid leave available to fathers and partners on a "use it or lose it" basis in order to incentivise shared care between couples (Work + Family Policy Roundtable 2022). Overseas evidence routinely shows that policies designed with a dedicated period for men and paid at relatively high income replacement levels result in greater take-up rates by fathers. For example, in Iceland the introduction of a reserved three months for fathers significantly shifted male behaviour, with 90 per cent using the leave (Koslowski & O'Brien 2022: 144; Haas & Rostgaard 2011). The restructuring of Germany's scheme to provide a dedicated period at high pay for fathers tripled men's use of leave (Koslowski & O'Brien 2022: 144). Affirming and non-stigmatising workplace cultures and policies also encourage men to use parental leave entitlements (Haas & Hwang 2019).

Level of pay

Ensuring an appropriate payment level is a critical tension in parental leave schemes, with various commentators and the ILO recommending a minimum of two-thirds of pre-birth earnings (Human Rights and Equal Opportunity Commission 2002b: 135). The Australian scheme is set at the National Minimum Wage which, as of November 2021, represented approximately 50 per cent of average full-time, adult, ordinary-time female earnings, and 42 per cent of average full-time, adult, ordinary-time male earnings (Whitehouse, Baird & Baxter 2022). This payment level has been criticised as being too low and contributing to the gender pay and earnings gap, a persistent problem in Australia. However, the flat-rate payment and having the payment set at a full-time level benefits women who work in lower paid jobs and part-time prior to birth, as these women may earn more from the parental leave payment than their pre-birth wage. In this respect, the scheme has an important redistributive element (Whitehouse & Nakazato 2021).

Superannuation

The lack of superannuation contributions in the federal government paid leave scheme is another major concern as it means women's superannuation balances are stalled while on parental leave, reducing total superannuation earnings and compounding the already negative impact of the gender pay gap on their lifetime earnings. Furthermore, not paying superannuation on a period of paid leave (as is done for annual leave) discriminates against women who make up the majority of users of the scheme and signals a low level of policy commitment to income equality (Work + Family Policy Roundtable 2022).

Private sector

Most policy attention and debate has focused on the government scheme, but important policy debates and developments are also occurring in the context of employer-provided schemes. In the private sector, debates about terminology have been prominent, particularly the move to eliminate eligibility distinctions between mothers and fathers, or "primary" and "secondary" carers (Jack & Jack 2022). While most employers do not offer more than 12 weeks, the leave is often paid at replacement wage or salary levels, rather than at minimum wage, and usually includes superannuation. Anecdotal reports also show that fathers are taking this leave, and available data on managerial take-up supports these reports (Workplace Gender Equality Agency 2022). However, these private sector developments tend to be concentrated in high-profile, large firms and are not available across the whole private sector workforce. They are also typically not available in areas that employ large proportions of women such as retail and hospitality, leading to further segmentation and inequities in entitlements, with some workers having access to generous parental leave policies while others rely solely on the government scheme.

3.6 The future and potential avenues for change

The introduction of the federal *Paid Parental Leave Act* in 2010 was acknowledged as a game-changer and the provision of paid parental leave in Australia is now recognised as an essential policy enabler of work and family reconciliation, as well as encouraging women's workforce participation. However, as we have indicated, it is far from perfect. In response to pressures to renovate the national system to better meet the needs of 21st-century family and work life and the Australian economy, the Albanese government announced significant changes to the scheme in its October 2022 Budget that will both simplify and extend the scheme. With the passing of the Paid Parental Leave Amendment (Improvements for Families and Gender Equality) Bill, from 1 July 2023, the distinction between leave for the primary carer (understood to be the mother) and Dad and Partner Pay will be removed and families will be able to access a total of 20 weeks paid parental leave. Two weeks are to be reserved each for the mother and the father and are non-transferable. The remaining 80 days (16 weeks) can be shared between the parents and used in increments of a day at a time, or blocks of time over a two-year period. The full 20 weeks will also be available to single parents. The duration of the scheme will then be increased each year by two weeks to 26 weeks by 2026. The reserved period for each parent is yet to be determined in the final 26-week model. In addition, the unpaid parental leave provision in the National Employment Standards has been amended to provide more flexibility. From April 2023, up to 100 days over 24 months can be used flexibly, the restriction on eight weeks simultaneous leave will be removed and pregnant employees will be able to take up to six weeks of the unpaid parental leave period before the birth.

These changes put Australia at a turning point in our parental leave system, introducing measures that better meet the multiple objectives of this foundational work and care policy. But there is clearly much more to be done. Even with the extension of the national system to 26 weeks, Australia will remain well below the average period of paid leave available to parents in other comparable economies, as shown in Figure 3.1. Twenty-six weeks is also too short for incentives designed to drive fathers to share the care of their young children more equally with their partners to be effective. To the extent that Australian women desire time to recover from birth and bond with their babies, and that many breastfeed, a leave period commensurate with the World Health Organization recommendation of 26 weeks of paid leave for

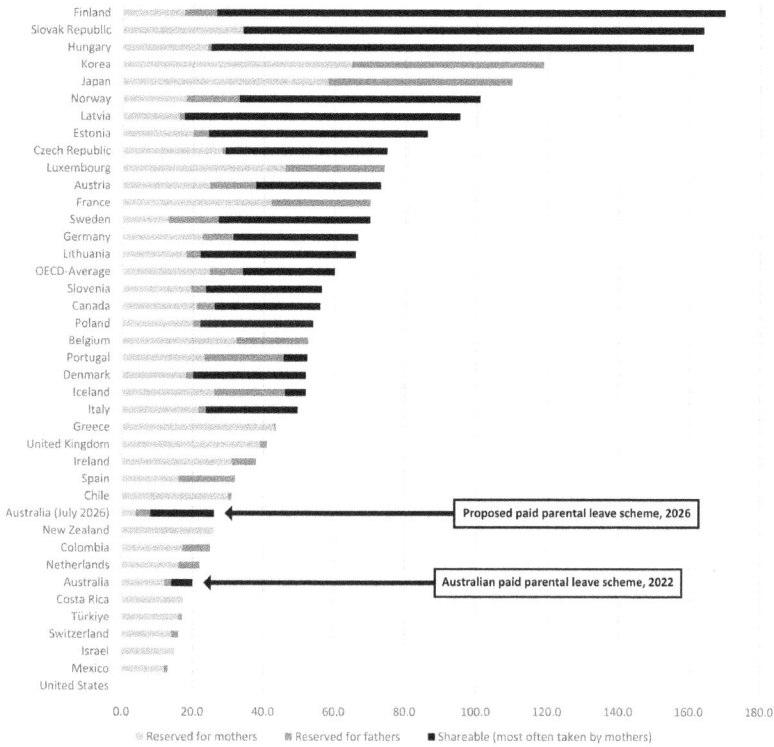

Figure 3.1 Duration of reserved and shareable parental leave entitlements, in weeks, 2021. Source: Adapted from OECD Family Policy Database (2021). Child-related leave, Table PF2.1 Key characteristics of parental leave systems. Available at https://www.oecd.org/els/family/database.htm.

working mothers should be the minimum available. It is hard to fit longer periods dedicated to father care into such a short time span.

A mix of social and economic factors contribute to a greater uptake of parental leave by fathers (Bergqvist & Saxonberg 2017), but two factors are widely recognised as having the potential to increase men's use of parental leave – a period of leave reserved for fathers' sole use and a high-income replacement level (see, e.g., World Policy Analysis Centre 2018: 17). For Australia to move towards a more equal sharing of work and care between parents, therefore, the total number of weeks of paid parental leave will have to be much longer and financial incentives need to be stronger.

One way to increase the payment levels to parents while on parental leave is for employers to increase their contribution, for example, by topping-up the minimum wage to full wage replacement and paying superannuation on the national scheme. However, incentives (other than their own business cases) or requirements for employers to top-up the national scheme or provide their own paid parental leave are noticeably absent under the current policy framework. At present, just 10 per cent of employers top-up the minimum parental leave pay to replacement wage rates and just under half of employers with 100 or more employees provide their own paid parental leave scheme, which is, however, typically at wage replacement levels (Baird et al. 2021). It is unclear how many smaller employers provide paid parental leave. Among the leading-practice companies, significant changes are occurring, particularly in expanding access to all parents. While these improvements in employer-provided schemes are welcome, they are not available to all workers and, as a result, contribute to greater labour market inequalities (Whitehouse et al. 2013).

Current policy settings leave Australia at risk of a two-tiered system of parental leave. The current enthusiasm in a number of large private sector corporations for gender-equal shared paid parental leave alongside a very modest national parental leave pay system is creating new inequalities in workers' access to paid parental leave. A small proportion of employees currently have access to state-of-the-art policies while the majority – especially women employed in sectors with limited provisions such as retail and hospitality, small private businesses or sectors that cannot provide more generous arrangements, as well as the self-employed and women in ongoing casual positions – are left with access to what could only be described as a residual national scheme. Improvements in the duration and level of income replacement and superannuation paid on the national scheme, as well as dedicated time for fathers and partners, are important policy challenges that must be addressed as part of the current focus of state and federal governments on gender equality in work and care. In addition, changes to the paid parental leave system must align with other social policies, most importantly a high-quality and well-resourced early childhood education and care system (see Chapter 4 in this volume). This is critical if parents are to be assured of quality and safe care of their infants when they return to work after parental leave.

References

Abbott, T. (2009). *Battlelines*. Carlton Vic: Melbourne University Press.
Australian Bureau of Statistics (2017). *Pregnancy and Employment Transitions, Australia, November 2017*. Cat. No. 49130. https://www.abs.gov.au/ausstats/abs@.nsf/mf/4913.0.
Australian Government Treasury (2020). *Retirement Income Review – Final Report*. https://bit.ly/4881zSZ.
Baird, M. (2005). Parental leave in Australia: the role of the industrial relations system. *Law in Context* 23(1): 45–64.
Baird, M. and Cutcher, L.(2005). One for the Father, One for the mother and one for the country: an examination of the construction of motherhood through the prism of paid maternity leave. *Hecate: An Interdisciplinary Journal of Women's Liberation* 31(2): 103–13.
Baird, M., Hamilton, M. and Constantin, V. (2021). Gender equality and paid parental leave in Australia: a decade of giant leaps or baby steps? *Journal of Industrial Relations* 63(4): 546–67.
Baird, M. and Heron, A. (2020). The life cycle of women's employment in Australia and inequality markers. In R.D. Lansbury, A. Johnson and D. van den Broek, eds. *Contemporary Issues in Work and Organisations: Actors and Institutions*, 42–56. Abingdon: Routledge.
Baird, M. and O'Brien, M. (2015). Dynamics of parental leave in Anglophone countries: the paradox of state expansion in the liberal welfare regimes. *Community, Work and Family* 18(2): 198–217.
Bergqvist, C. and Saxonberg, S. (2017). The state as a norm-builder? the take-up of parental leave in Norway and Sweden. *Social Policy and Administration* 51: 1470–87. https://doi.org/10.1111/spol.12251.
Brennan, D.J. (2009). A late delivery? the politics of maternity leave in Australia. In S. Kamerman and P. Moss, eds. *The Politics of Parental Leave Policies: Children, Parenting, Gender and the Labour Market*, 33–50. Bristol: The Policy Press. https://doi.org/10.1332/policypress/9781847420671.001.0001.

Broadway, B., Kalb, G., McVicar, D. and Martin, B. (2020). The impact of paid parental leave on labor supply and employment outcomes in Australia. *Feminist Economics* 26(3): 30–65.

Cooklin, A.R., Rowe, H.J. and Fisher, J.R.W. (2012). Paid parental leave supports breastfeeding and mother-infant relationship: a prospective investigation of maternal postpartum employment. *Australian and New Zealand Journal of Public Health* 36(3): 249–56.

Department of Families, Housing, Community Services and Indigenous Affairs (2012). *Annual Report, 2011–12.* https://bit.ly/47JnQqD.

Department of Social Services (2021). *Annual Report 2020–21.* https://bit.ly/41eQXiV.

Department of Social Services (2020). *Annual Report, 2019–20.* https://bit.ly/3v15zGH.

Dobrotić, I. and Blum, S. (2020). Inclusiveness of parental leave benefits in twenty-one European countries: measuring social and gender inequalities in leave eligibility. *Social Politics* 27(3): 588–614.

Grattan, M. (2015). Abbott ditches signature policy as his disapproval soars. *The Conversation*, 2 February. https://bit.ly/47MeTNb.

Haas, L. and Hwang, C.P. (2019). Policy is not enough – the influence of the gendered workplace on fathers' use of parental leave in Sweden. *Community, Work and Family* 22(1): 58–76.

Haas, L. and Rostgaard, T. (2011). Fathers' rights to paid parental leave in the Nordic countries: consequences for the gendered division of leave. *Community, Work and Family* 14(2): 177–95.

Human Rights and Equal Opportunity Commission (2002a). *Valuing Parenthood: Options for a Paid Maternity Leave Scheme.* Sydney: Human Rights and Equal Opportunity Commission.

Human Rights and Equal Opportunity Commission (2002b). *A Time to Value: Proposal for a National Paid Maternity Leave Scheme.* Sydney: Human Rights and Equal Opportunity Commission.

Jack, M. and Jack, D. (2022). *Bridging the Work and Family Divide.* Parents@Work and UNICEF Australia. https://bit.ly/41tjwtj.

Kladpor, M. (2013–14). Abolishing the Baby Bonus. https://bit.ly/3R5AcCc.

Koslowski, A., Blum, S., Dobrotić, I., Kaufman, G. and Moss, P. eds (2021). *International Review of Leave Policies and Research 2021.* https://www.leavenetwork.org/annual-review-reports/archive-reviews/.

Koslowski, A. and O'Brien, M. (2022). Fathers and family leave policies: what public policy can do to support families. In M. Grau Grau, M. las Heras Maestro and H. Riley Bowles, eds. *Engaged Fatherhood for Men, Families and Gender Equality*, 141–52. Cham, Switzerland: Springer.

Lauzon-Guillain, B., Thierry, X., Bois, C., Bournez, M., Davisse-Paturet, C., Dufourg, M. et al. (2019). Maternity or parental leave and breastfeeding duration: results from the ELFE cohort. *Maternal and Child Nutrition* 15(4): 1–13.

Martin, B., Baird, M., Brady, M., Broadway, B., Hewitt, B., Kalb, et al. (2014). *Paid Parental Leave Evaluation: Final Report.* Canberra: Department of Social Services. https://bit.ly/3RgBKJA.

Martin, B., Hewitt, B., Baird, M., Baxter, J., Heron, A., Whitehouse, G.et al. (2012). *Paid Parental Leave Evaluation: Phase 1,* Occasional Paper No. 44. Canberra: Department of Families, Housing, Community Services and Indigenous Affairs. https://bit.ly/3RbtVEZ.

Mirkovic, K.R., Perrine, C.G. and Scanlon, K.S. (2016). Paid maternity leave and breastfeeding outcomes. *Birth: Issues in Perinatal Care* 43(3): 233–9.

OECD (2012). *Closing the Gender Gap: Act Now.* Paris: OECD Publishing. https://doi.org/10.1787/9789264179370-en.

OECD Family Database (2022). *Key Characteristics of Parental Leave Systems.* https://www.oecd.org/els/soc/PF2_1_Parental_leave_systems.pdf.

Productivity Commission (2009). *Paid Parental Leave: Support for Parents with Newborn Children.* Inquiry report. Canberra: Australian Government.

Queensland Government (2020). *Paid Parental Leave,* Directive 05/20. https://bit.ly/3uS5W6n.

Ruhm, C. (1998). The economic consequences of parental leave mandates: lessons from Europe. *The Quarterly Journal of Economics* 113(1): 285–317.

Van Niel, M.S., Bhatia, R., Riano, N.S., de Faria, L., Catapano-Friedman, L., Ravven, S. et al. (2019). The impact of paid maternity leave on the mental and physical health of mothers and children: a review of the literature and policy implications. *Harvard Review of Psychiatry* 28(2): 113–26.

Whitehouse, G., Baird, M. and Baxter, J.A. (2022). Australia country note. In A. Koslowski, S. Blum, I. Dobrotić, G. Kaufman and P. Moss, eds. *International Review of Leave Policies and Research 2022.* https://bit.ly/3tdkZHa.

Whitehouse, G., Baird M. and Baxter J.A. (2021). Australia country note. In A. Koslowski, S. Blum, I. Dobrotić, G. Kaufman and P. Moss, eds. *International Review of Leave Policies and Research 2021.* https://bit.ly/3tdkZHa.

Whitehouse, G., Baird, M. Diamond, C. and Hosking A. (2006). *The Parental Leave in Australia Survey: November 2006 Report.* https://bit.ly/3Gwe3Dg.

Whitehouse, G., Baird, M. and Morrissey, S. (2022). Legacies of an antipodean model? parenting leave policy trajectories in Australia and New Zealand. In I. Dobrotić, S. Blum and A. Koslowski, eds. *Research Handbook on Leave Policy,* 245–57. Cheltenham: Edward Elgar Publishing.

Whitehouse, G. and Brady M. (2019). Parental leave, social inequalities and the future of work: possibilities and constraints within the Australian policy framework. *Labour and Industry* 29(3): 257–72.

Whitehouse, G., Hewitt, B., Martin, B. and Baird, M. (2013). Employer-paid maternity leave in Australia: A comparison of uptake and duration in 2005 and 2010. *Australian Journal of Labour Economics* 16(3): 311–27.

Whitehouse, G. and Nakazato, H. (2021). Dimensions of social equality in parental leave policy design: comparing Australia and Japan. *Social Inclusion* 9(2): 288–99.

Wood, D., Emslie, O. and Griffiths, K. (2021). *Dad Days: How More Gender-Equal Parental Leave Could Improve the Lives of Australian Families*. Melbourne: Grattan Institute.

Work + Family Policy Roundtable (2022). *Election Benchmarks Scorecard 2022*. https://bit.ly/3Rgy4Yx.

Work + Family Policy Roundtable (2015). Government attack on new mothers. Press release, 12 May. https://bit.ly/3Rf7WwP.

Workplace Gender Equality Agency (2022). *Australia's Gender Equality Scorecard*.WGEA Scorecard 2022: The state of gender equality in Australia | WGEA.https://bit.ly/3Gx6n8z.

Workplace Gender Equality Agency Data Explorer. Accessed August 2022: http://data.wgea.gov.au/industries/1#carers_content.

World Policy Analysis Centre (2018). *Paid Parental Leave: A Detailed Look at Approaches Across OECD Countries*. Los Angeles: World Policy Analysis Centre.

4
Early childhood education and care: Policy renewal for strong foundations

Elizabeth Hill, Elizabeth Adamson and Deborah Brennan

4.1 Introduction

Early childhood education and care (ECEC) has been a contested policy area for decades. The COVID-19 crisis brought underlying tensions and contradictions to the fore, exposing both the fragility of the system and its inability to meet the needs of all stakeholders: children, parents, ECEC workers, providers and government. Following the election of the Albanese Labor government in May 2022, the Treasurer requested the Productivity Commission to inquire into the sector, acknowledging that ECEC is "an essential part of Australia's education system and is integral to Australia's economic prosperity as a powerful lever for increasing workforce participation". Expressing a commitment to " universal, affordable ECEC in the great tradition of universal Medicare and universal superannuation" the Treasurer asked the Commission to give equal weight to children's education and development and to adult workforce participation (Chalmers 2023).[1]

---

[1] In February 2023, Deborah Brennan was appointed an Associate Commissioner to the Productivity Commissioner in order to co-lead this inquiry.

This chapter focuses on the need for a strong system of *formal* child care, while also recognising the crucial role played by *informal* care. We consider the key elements of Australia's ECEC policy architecture, paying particular attention to government funding and private sector market mechanisms. These are the components of ECEC that determine wages, prices (fees) and access, and where progressive reform could be most effective. We also address the critical question of where children's interests are situated in ECEC service delivery.

In 2021, more than 13,500 services across Australia were approved to deliver formal ECEC as part of the Commonwealth Child Care Subsidy (CCS) scheme, which is the primary source of public funding support for parents. The CCS is generally paid directly to providers to decrease the out-of-pocket costs to families (Productivity Commission 2022). Centre-based Long Day Care (LDC) represented 62.5 per cent of these services, followed by Outside School Hours Care (OSHC) at 34.1 per cent (Department of Education 2021). Almost 1.4 million children aged 0 to 12 years attended CCS-funded services, including 46.4 per cent of 0–5-year-olds, and 32 per cent of 6–12-year-olds (Department of Education 2021). Unlike other forms of social and educational infrastructure in Australia, such as public schools, ECEC for children under school age is delivered via a "quasi-market" system (King & Meagher 2009). Quasi-markets are those in which government funding is the main source of purchasing power, mostly via public subsidies that consumers use to choose among competing public or private services. The existence of a quasi-market in ECEC means that formal services are provided by a mix of government, not-for-profit and for-profit providers, each of which can access the CCS. Of all Commonwealth approved providers of ECEC services, 51 per cent are private for-profit and 34 per cent are private not-for-profit. The remaining 15 per cent are a mix of state/territory-run or independent schools (Australian Children's Education and Care Quality Authority 2022a).

Complexities in the provision of ECEC services and its funding are accompanied by tensions over the policy objectives of ECEC: providing early learning and care for children, and supporting the employment of workers, especially mothers (Adamson & Brennan 2014; Penn 2011). These often-conflicting goals are embedded deep within the policy architecture, leaving parents to negotiate complex eligibility guidelines and public subsidy rules. Targeted eligibility criteria prioritise access to subsidised services for the children of parents who are employed or in training, often leaving the early learning needs of the most vulnerable children unmet. Federal government efforts to contain expenditure on services limits the ability of the ECEC workforce to achieve wages that reflect the complexity and responsibility of their work. Meanwhile, the inability to access appropriate and affordable ECEC is the main obstacle women face in starting a new job or increasing their hours of work (Australian Bureau of Statistics 2020).

The COVID-19 pandemic that emerged in 2020 exposed and intensified the longstanding structural vulnerabilities, complexity and contested nature of ECEC policy. Lockdowns highlighted problems with the funding model for formal services that saw the federal government forced to deliver emergency support to keep providers afloat.[2] In the first lockdown, between April and July 2020, formal ECEC was made free for all parents (Department of Education, Skills and Employment 2020). However, the workforce did not receive adequate support and came under acute pressure with each wave of the pandemic. Many dedicated educators left the sector, overwhelmed by ever-changing government health and financial aid regulations, the need to provide intense support to families impacted by the pandemic and their own concerns about exposure to the virus, all in return for low wages. The workforce crisis that was building pre-pandemic intensified, with many leaving the sector permanently (United Workers Union 2021a).

With Australia's ECEC system now at a breaking point, this chapter evaluates the current crisis in its historical and contemporary context and seeks to identify pathways for positive change. We begin by providing a brief history of Australia's approach to ECEC policy to explain the current policy architecture for ECEC funding, workforce and quality. We then discuss current policy tensions and avenues for change, arguing that post-pandemic recovery provides a historic opportunity to think differently about ECEC and its role in society

---

2   The timing and generosity of these emergency support packages varied between 2020 and 2021 and by state/territory depending on the severity of the lockdown.

and the economy. With the right policy settings and new investment, the ECEC system could be redesigned to build human capabilities and reduce inequalities of gender, race and class as well as providing support for parental workforce participation. Policy debates both within Australia and internationally suggest that ECEC policy renewal in a post-pandemic world can contribute to a new social contract in which everyone has the right to care and be cared for over the life course, with profound spillover benefits for society and the economy.

4.2 Brief history and context of the policy in Australia

Children's access to ECEC has increased dramatically since the 1970s when the Commonwealth first began to provide funding to community-based not-for-profit services. Despite the growth in service provision, there are marked inequities in access to Commonwealth supported services. Those most likely to miss out on ECEC services include children from low-income families (Australian Bureau of Statistics 2018: Table 4), Aboriginal and Torres Strait Islander children (SNAICC 2021), children with disability, children living in rural and remote areas and children from non-English speaking backgrounds (Productivity Commission 2021: Table 3A.12). Emerging evidence shows that it is children from disadvantaged circumstances who are the least likely to have access to the high-quality services that would positively affect their life chances (Cloney et al. 2016). Australia lags behind comparable countries in failing to offer any guarantees of service provision, as is the case in France and most Scandinavian countries (Gromada & Richardson 2021). We also rank poorly compared with other OECD economies in terms of public investment in ECEC: as of 2017, Australia spent approximately 0.6 per cent of GDP on early childhood education and care for children aged 0 to 5, compared with New Zealand's 1.0 per cent, Iceland's 1.8 per cent and an OECD average of just over 0.7 per cent (OECD 2021). This means New Zealand spends almost double and Iceland more than three times as much as Australia per child annually on early learning and care, leaving Australian parents to cover some of the highest child care fees in the world (Gromada & Richardson 2021). Australia's generally low level of public support for policies that help parents care for young children[3] is reflected in our overall ranking of 37 out of 41 wealthy economies in UNICEF's 2021 report on child care (Gromada & Richardson 2021: 7).

Contested views about the appropriate balance of responsibility for children between families, governments, non-profit providers and markets underpin the politics of ECEC. The picture is further complicated by a lack of clarity about the objectives of ECEC and the presence of multiple stakeholders seeking to advance their own interests. These pressures intensified in the early 1990s when public subsidies were extended to services provided by for-profit businesses (Newberry & Brennan 2013). This "radical marketisation" of education and care services for young children means ECEC is shaped by the often competing philosophies and imperatives of non-profit and for-profit providers in addition to the complexities of federalism. Child care is now big business, with several large providers listed on the stock exchange (United Workers Union 2021b; Hill & Wade 2018). Although non-profit providers continue to play a significant role in the delivery of services, the sector as a whole is heavily marketised, with market principles determining the location of new services and the allocation of subsidies. As a result, ECEC is constructed as a commodity to be bought and sold, rather than a community service or an essential element of social and economic infrastructure.

In recent years, new issues, or new formulations of old issues, have become the subject of debate and contestation. For example, advocacy in the 1970s highlighted the ECEC needs of culturally and linguistically diverse families, an issue that has received renewed attention following the rapid expansion in temporary migrant work since 2010. This demographic shift has highlighted the critical question of how to support the children of workers on temporary visas who are barred from accessing federal child care subsidies and who find it difficult to access informal grandparent care due to migration restrictions (Hamilton et al. 2021). On the inequitable access of Aboriginal and Torres Strait Islander children to ECEC, First Nations organisations are

---

3   The UNICEF League Table ranks each country on eight indicators grouped into four dimensions: leave, access, quality and affordability of child care.

playing a leading role in framing understandings of how best to support their children and families (SNAICC 2021).

4.3 Current policy architecture

The current ECEC system is shaped by a range of laws, policies and regulations that determine funding and access, ensure quality regulation of services, and determine the pay and employment conditions of workers. Less directly, tax and social security policies interact with child care subsidies in problematic ways (see Chapter 7), while migration policy contributes to the availability of formal and informal workers across the sector (Howe, Charlesworth & Brennan 2019). This makes for a highly complex system involving all levels of government as well as the private sector and non-government organisations. It is at the intersection of these policies that parents try to reconcile their work and care responsibilities and the early learning needs of their children.

As in most OECD countries, early childhood education and care in Australia is provided in a mix of formal and informal settings (see Table 4.1). *Formal* care is funded, or partly subsidised, and subject to government regulation at the state/territory or federal level (Rutter & Evans 2012). Formal care services can be provided in centre-based settings such as Long Day Care, Preschool and Outside School Hours Care, or in private homes like Family Day Care or In Home Care. *Informal* care, on the other hand, is generally not subsidised and is not subject to regulatory oversight. It can be provided by family members (such as grandparents), neighbours or friends, and can be paid or unpaid. Children's use of formal and informal care has changed over the past two decades. While some caution must be used in comparisons due to methodological changes, key indicators show that from 1996 to 2017, the proportion of children aged 0 to 11 years using only formal care increased from 9 per cent to 15 per cent, while the proportion using informal care exclusively decreased from 31 per cent to 19 per cent. Around half of all children aged 0 to 12 years use some form of non-parental care (Australian Bureau of Statistics 2018). Most families use a combination of formal and informal care.

Table 4.1 Structure and funding of the Australian ECEC system

Type of care	Typical age range	Formal or informal	Funding support
Long Day Care (LDC)	6 months to 5 years	Formal	Commonwealth Child Care Subsidy (CCS)
Family Day Care (FDC)	6 months to 12 years	Formal	Commonwealth Child Care Subsidy (CCS)
In Home Care	6 months to 12 years	Formal	Commonwealth Child Care Subsidy (CCS)
Preschool	3 to 5 years	Formal	State/territory and Commonwealth funding
Outside School Hours Care (OSHC)	5 to 12 years	Formal	Commonwealth Child Care Subsidy (CCS)
Grandparent care	0 to 12 years	Informal	None
Other family and friends	0 to 12 years	Informal	None
Nanny or au pair	0 to 12 years	Informal	None

In 2017, grandparent care was the most common type of child care arrangement in Australia, with almost 900,000 children aged 0 to 12 years cared for by a grandparent. Grandparent care is particularly common for children under 2 years, and school-aged children between 5 and 8 years (Australian Bureau of Statistics 2018: Table 1). In contrast, children aged 2 to 3 years are more likely to attend formal services, with approximately 50 per cent of this age group attending long day care (Australian Bureau of Statistics 2018: Table 1). Approximately 87 per cent of all children in the year before school attend a preschool program in either a government or non-government preschool (i.e. Catholic or private school), or in a long day care setting where the program is delivered by a qualified teacher (Productivity Commission 2022: Table 3A.17). Migrant families face a complex mix of opportunities and constraints, depending on their particular circumstances. Many choose grandparent care over formal options because of their wish to strengthen intergenerational and cultural connections; others turn to the grandparents or other family members due to lack of access to appropriate, affordable formal services. If grandparents live primarily in another country (as is very common in multicultural Australia), migration, health and social security rules constrain their ability to visit

Australia and provide care support to their children and grandchildren. Visas are limited, costly and hard to obtain (Hamilton et al. 2021), making grandparent care difficult to sustain as a regular form of care. For some families (migrant and non-migrant) with adequate resources, nannies and au pairs may offer another choice. Au pair work, in particular, is a complex type of ECEC that crosses the formal and informal domains and has recently attracted both policy and researchattention (Berg & Meagher 2018).

Funding for formal ECEC services

The funding and administrative arrangements for ECEC are extremely complex. Responsibility for funding and regulation crosses state/ territory and federal jurisdictions and differs according to the type of care. As discussed above, some of these complexities are rooted in historical funding legacies and outdated ideological approaches to preschool and early learning, while others emerged as part of the "radical marketisation" of child care in the 1990s and 2000s that saw corporate services come to dominate the sector (Newberry & Brennan 2013).

The Commonwealth government provides funding for long day care, family day care and out of school hours care services, while state and territory governments fund preschool services (see Table 4.1) (Productivity Commission 2022: Table 3.2). There is no public funding for informal care services. Federal support for approved ECEC services is delivered through the Child Care Subsidy (CCS) and is determined by the income and other characteristics of families. The CCS is generally paid directly to the provider, who passes it on to families as a fee reduction. Eligibility criteria for the CCS include strict residency and work or study activity tests, with recipients limited to parents who are employed or studying and are citizens or holders of specific visa types. The amount of CCS available to parents is calculated with reference to a federal government benchmark fee that varies by service type.[4] The subsidy varies according to household income, parental

---

4   The benchmark fee is $12.74/hour for Long Day Care, $11.80 for Family Day Care and $12.74 for Outside School Hours Care (2021–22).

"activity" as measured by hours of work or study, and the number of children in the family who participate in ECEC. Subsidy rules have varied over the years. In July 2023, the CCS rules changed again, when the federal Albanese Labor government introduced a higher CCS rate and income threshold. These changes were designed to deliver "cheaper child care" (*Family Assistance Legislation Amendment (Cheaper Child Care) Act 2022* (Cth)), increasing the subsidy rate from 85 per cent to 90 per cent of the benchmark fee for families with annual incomes under AU$80,000. The subsidy rate decreases by 1 per cent for every $5,000 increase in income, tapering to 20 per cent CCS for families earning up to $530,000 a year. The higher income cut-off is a significant increase from the $356,756 threshold in 2022–23. Parents must pay any unsubsidised portion of the benchmark fee, plus any amount charged by the provider above the benchmark fee, directly to the provider. Until 2021, families earning over $190,015 per year faced a cap of $10,655 on the annual amount of CCS they could receive. This cap was abolished in December 2021 and the changes backdated to the start of the 2021–22 financial year. As of 7 March 2022, families with more than one child aged five or younger receive a higher rate of subsidy for additional children, capped at 95 per cent.

Preschools are funded by state, territory and Commonwealth governments. Since 2008, the Preschool Reform Funding Agreement has provided Commonwealth funding for all states and territories to deliver 15 hours of preschool per week per child by a qualified teacher in the year before formal schooling. In 2020, New South Wales and Victoria began to extend additional funding for preschool for three-year-olds, focusing initially on children from vulnerable backgrounds. In 2022, New South Wales and Victoria committed to delivering five full days of free preschool in the year before school for all children over the next 10 years (New South Wales Government 2022; Victorian Government 2022). Other states and territories are running pilot programs or have extended preschools for three-year-olds to vulnerable communities and families (Lucas 2021).

In contrast to the state-based initiatives for preschool, the demand-driven design of the Commonwealth CCS and the strict work or study activity test create real and perceived barriers for children from low-income and other vulnerable groups. Parents who have casual, insecure and unpredictable work patterns find it difficult to navigate the CCS system, not least because it requires parents to predict their future work and income. The CCS is paid based on parents' estimated income and is adjusted at the end of the financial year once actual income is known, sometimes giving rise to a debt to be paid to the Australian Taxation Office. The uncertainty embedded within the CCS system imposes an administrative barrier for those in precarious or non-standard employment and those looking for employment, with the consequence that vulnerable children who are most likely to benefit from high-quality early learning environments are the most likely to miss out on access to such services (The Front Project 2019). The CCS also interacts in complex ways with the tax and benefit systems and creates financial disincentives for women to increase their workforce participation or accept a promotion (Stewart 2021). We discuss this issue briefly in the section below and it is explored in detail in Chapter 7 in this volume.

The limited scope and scale of government-supported flexible ECEC options[5] means families with non-standard or unpredictable work (such as health and emergency service shift workers), or those with multiple children, have very limited ECEC options and often turn to babysitters, nannies or au pairs who operate outside the formal ECEC system. Since COVID-19, the supply of au pairs, often sourced from international students or young people on Working Holiday Maker visas, has declined drastically, putting further pressure on families requiring flexible care (Emery 2021). Evidence of poor working conditions among workers in this part of the ECEC system has also raised concerns about its effectiveness and sustainability (Oishi & Ono 2020; Berg & Meagher 2018).

Finally, Australia's ECEC system is detached from other policies that address the care of young children such as paid parental leave (see Chapter 3). Funding and time limits on the national system of paid parental leave, alongside limited access to timely enrolment in ECEC, especially for very young children aged six months to two years, leaves many families facing long waiting periods for access to formal care

---

5   An exception is a small, targeted In Home Care Program for families unable to use Long Day Care.

services and the challenge of negotiating the "gap" between the end of paid parental leave and access to suitable ECEC. This gap in support for the care of young children is a particular feature of current policy settings and points to the need for a new "joined-up" approach to care for children from birth to the early years of school. This would provide a longer period of paid leave for parents of very young children and ensure easy access to high-quality care options that can support parents' return to paid work. This is both a policy design and funding challenge. Some advocacy groups have begun to bring these areas together. The Centre for Policy Development, for example, has called for an integrated system of early childhood development including a longer period of paid parental leave that can be shared between partners, a guarantee of access to three days a week of quality early education for every child before the commencement of school, and greater community and health support for families (Centre for Policy Development 2021).

Workforce and quality regulation

The ECEC workforce is highly feminised, and highly reliant on migrant workers. Before the pandemic, more than 95 per cent of ECEC workers were female and 35 per cent were born overseas, with the majority (79 per cent) of the overseas born from countries in which English is not the main language (Eastman et al. 2019). Informal and familial care is also overwhelmingly performed by women (id.community 2022). The formal ECEC workforce is well trained, with qualification requirements of educators set by the National Quality Standard. Established in 2012, the National Quality Standard is a positive feature of the Australian ECEC system, setting the quality standard for the sector and acting as a guide for parents. This includes professional qualifications for workers and minimum staff:child ratios as well as other health and safety standards. Workers in formal ECEC services must have, at a minimum, completed or be working towards a Certificate III in Early Childhood Education and Care. Additional regulations stipulate the requirement to employ university-trained early childhood teachers. The introduction of the National Quality Standard has seen significant improvement in the quality of the ECEC sector, with 86 per cent of approved services rated as meeting or exceeding the National Quality Standard (Australian Children's Education and Care Quality Authority 2021a) and 76 per cent of primary contact staff in government-approved child care services holding Certificate III qualifications or above (Productivity Commission 2022: Table 3A.29).

However, professionalisation of the sector has not translated into better wages or good careers for the ECEC workforce. Wages across all types of ECEC services are low, with early childhood educators reporting median incomes approximately half that of the total workforce (Eastman, et al. 2019) and degree-qualified teachers in long day care settings earning approximately 65 per cent of their counterparts in preschool and school settings (Australian Children's Education and Care Quality Authority 2019, authors' calculations). Divergence in pay across provider settings makes retention of the most highly qualified teachers in long day care difficult (McDonald et al. 2018) and low wages across the sector are routinely identified as the primary cause of low retention rates, with many workers reporting they cannot afford to pursue a career in ECEC (Thorpe et al. 2020). Low wages have a cumulative negative impact on women's superannuation and economic security in retirement, an issue that is more pronounced in private for-profit providers (United Workers Union 2021b: 9). Informal au pair and nanny services are not subject to the same minimum standards as formal ECEC services and the lack of regulation for informal care remains a concern for both the quality of care for children and the employment conditions of workers (Berg & Meagher 2018).

4.4 Current policy tensions and debates

Current ECEC policy architecture reflects several critical tensions that limit the ability of ECEC services to meet the work and care needs of families with different needs. Debates about the policy goals of ECEC remain unresolved, leaving Australian services among the most expensive in the world, as well as being inflexible and often poorly suited to large numbers of parents who have unpredictable work schedules. The term "child care deserts" has been coined to describe large parts of Australia, particularly rural and regional locations and low socio-economic urban areas, where child care is effectively unavailable (Hurley et al. 2022). Inadequate government funding for formal services ensures low pay, making long-term careers in the sector difficult to sustain for workers and workforce planning a challenge for providers. The current system is extremely complex for parents and service providers to navigate and the pandemic has highlighted and exacerbated each of these policy tensions.

Aim and purpose of ECEC

Australian ECEC policy settings are hamstrung by competing rationales: should ECEC primarily be delivered as a system of early learning and care for all children, or as a support for women's labour supply and government workforce agenda? In principle, both outcomes could be achieved (as they are in some Scandinavian countries), but the existence of a strict work or study activity test to determine access to Commonwealth subsidies means that priority is given to ECEC as a support for workforce participation rather than as a public good or a right for children and families. This policy persists despite the large body of Australian and international scholarship on the benefits of public investment in the early years for child development, social inclusion and intergenerational equality (PricewaterhouseCoopers 2019; Pascoe & Brennan 2017; Thrive By Five 2017) and the long-term economic benefits that derive from ECEC's impact on school readiness and future employment success (Heckman 2012), especially for children from First Nations communities and disadvantaged households (Sydenham 2019). Access to Commonwealth subsidies for ECEC continues to be largely premised on participation in work or preparation for work, with a residual safety net program for the most disadvantaged. However, limits on public funding mean that the high out-of-pocket cost for many parents using subsidised services, lack of flexibility and complex interactions between the ECEC and tax and transfer systems leave families (and women in particular) unable to access the ECEC services they require to work the hours they prefer. Lack of clarity about the purpose of ECEC has led to the development of a system that does not work for women, parents or children.

The failure of the system to support families to make their own choices about work and care has seen ECEC become a major political issue in recent federal elections. This enhanced political priority reflects the broad consensus developed over the past decade between business, civil society, ECEC professionals and parents about the social and economic benefits of additional investment in a public system of universal, affordable or free ECEC (Centre for Policy Development 2021; The Parenthood 2021a; The Front Project 2019; Thrive by Five 2017). Notably, the focus of this broad coalition of advocates is not only on women's labour supply, but also very clearly on the education and care benefits for young children and gender equality. In the pandemic context, the rationale for additional investment in ECEC strengthened in 2022 with new investment a key election promise of the incoming federal Albanese Labor government after the May 2022 election.

Cost

Despite significantly increased public expenditure on subsidies for formal ECEC over the past 20 years,[6] Australia has one of the most expensive systems globally, ranking 34 out of 41 countries in family affordability for child care (Gromada & Richardson 2021:7). Currently, the average fee for 10 hours of long day care (before subsidy) is $105 a day. The cost of child care depends on the number of days per week that children attend, and the family income, which affects the CCS amount. However, the Mitchell Institute calculated that, in 2020, a family with two children in long day care for 30 hours per week spent between 9 per cent and 12 per cent of weekly disposable income on child care, after the subsidy and depending on their income (Noble & Hurley 2021: Table 2). Using an international benchmark that sets a child care affordability threshold at equal to no more than 7 per cent of household disposable income, the same study found that child care is unaffordable for almost 40 per cent of families in Australia (Noble & Hurley 2021). The high out-of-pocket cost limits the ability of many

---

6   Since 2000, Commonwealth subsidies for ECEC have increased from $1.04 billion to $12.7 billion in 2023–24. Forward estimates show the CCS increasing to almost $15 billion by 2026–27.

households to access appropriate ECEC services and highlights the tension between Australia's quasi-market system and the provision of affordable services. The high cost of ECEC for many parents is a specific and structural feature of the Australian system.

Inflexible provision and access

The primary rationale of Australia's system of ECEC is the promotion of parental workforce participation. However, services and subsidies do not align well with the employment conditions of many parents and the structure of contemporary labour markets. This creates tension between service supply and demand. Most ECEC services run between 7am and 6pm and require parents to commit to regular days and hours of use. This does not align with many parents' working schedules or needs. Lack of flexibility in the ECEC system has long been identified as a problem for nurses, emergency service workers and police, but the mismatch between the hours formal services run and the employment conditions of many parents has rapidly extended into a range of other sectors. Ad hoc changes to rosters and just-in-time scheduling of work hours in many low-wage, insecure and highly feminised sectors such as retail, hospitality, aged care and disability care render most formal ECEC services unfit for purpose (Cortis et al. 2021). Employment time insecurity and fragmentation, alongside lack of access to suitable ECEC, combine to create serious limits on women's economic security, career progression and children's care (Cortis et al. 2021).

Low-paid workforce

Low wages for ECEC workers are a perennial problem for the sector, whose income is from two main sources: the Child Care Subsidy provided by the federal government and parent "gap" fees. As the primary funder, the Commonwealth is effectively the lead employer. But limits on funding lock ECEC workers into low wages that in turn drive the low retention rates that have produced a workforce crisis (Australian Children's Education and Care Quality Authority 2021b; Jackson 2020; Thorpe et al. 2020; McDonald et al. 2018). This has only deepened with the additional pressures imposed by the COVID-19 pandemic (Dent 2021). The Australian Children's Education and Care Quality Authority (2021b) reports that sixty per cent of the workforce have less than six years' experience in the ECEC sector. Lack of retention and career development for educators in the sector has implications for the quality of the education and care delivered in services, as high-quality care is best delivered by a stable and well-trained workforce (OECD 2020). Tensions between the funding model, wages, retention and high-quality service delivery make the funding of professional wages for ECEC workers a key nexus in the system. Union and community campaigns for higher wages for ECEC workers that reflect the skill and value they provide to children, families, the community and the economy have gathered momentum in recent years (The Parenthood 2021b; The Front Project 2020). But who will pay? The Commonwealth is resistant, employers' initial interest in providing in-house ECEC services has waned since the early 2000s due to tax and regulatory disincentives, and parents are already paying too much as international comparisons show. A fundamental redesign of Commonwealth investment and funding in ECEC is required to deliver fair wages and conditions for educators without increasing the costs faced by parents. Further, since the private market is unable to deliver equitable access to quality ECEC, especially for children in disadvantaged circumstances, governments will need to become more interventionist to boost supply.

Complexity in design

The complex service system and subsidy rules that characterise ECEC in Australia, in combination with the tax and transfer system, create perverse incentives and tensions for families in their calculations about who works and who cares. The amount of subsidy a family is eligible for is calculated by referring to parental workforce participation, household income, days of ECEC used and number of children in ECEC. As household income increases from doing more hours of work or taking a higher paid job, the CCS is reduced, as are other social security and transfer payments (such as family tax benefits). Interactions between the CCS, tax and transfer payments produce a high effective marginal tax rate (EMTR) or workforce disincentive rate

(WDR) calculated as the proportion of a second earner's gross take-home pay from an extra day's paid work that is lost to tax, net child care costs and reduction in other benefits (see Chapter 7 in this volume; Wood, et al. 2020). High workforce disincentive rates are a structural feature of Australia's highly targeted tax and transfer system and are a perennial concern for policymakers (Whiteford, Redmond & Adamson 2011). Faced by high workforce disincentive rates, some families seek informal ECEC arrangements to supplement or replace formal services. However, informal care is poorly supported in current policy settings, leading to additional tensions for parents. Grandparents provide essential family care, but many older workers find it difficult to secure the kind of flexible work that would enable them to provide regular child care to grandchildren (see Chapter 5 in this volume; Hamilton & Suthersan 2020). Some grandparents leave work altogether to cover the child care needs of their adult children, thus compromising their own economic security (Hamilton & Suthersan 2020). Accessing grandparent care for workers on temporary visas and longer term migrants is much more complicated (Hamilton et al 2021), and while au pairs are often seen as a convenient and affordable informal alternative, visa rules and ECEC regulations do not protect au pairs as workers or establish a minimum quality of care for children (Berg & Meagher 2018).

A pandemic highlights tensions

Each of the policy tensions outlined above has been made more acute during the pandemic, as public health orders and the economic downturns wreaked havoc on households' work–care arrangements while also threatening the viability of formal service providers. The reliance of the ECEC sector on Commonwealth funding meant that when the pandemic hit, the federal government had no choice but to provide emergency funding to keep services operating for the children of essential workers. The initial 2020 emergency package did what the government had always said was not possible – provide ECEC at no cost to families (Prime Minister and Minister for Education 2020). Workforce support was provided through the national JobKeeper program, but many ECEC workers were ineligible for the payment either because they had worked for their employer for less than 12 months or because they held a temporary visa (Australian Treasury 2020; Howe, Charlesworth & Brennan 2019; Eastman, Charlesworth & Hill 2018). In other words, the insecurity of their employment excluded them from Commonwealth financial support. These emergency arrangements lasted for just three months before a graduated return to the pre-pandemic system began on 13 July 2020 (Klapdor 2020). In 2021, the federal government was much slower to provide emergency support during the July–November lockdowns, eventually implementing a Viability Support Package on 23 August 2021.[7] The 2021 package granted emergency funds to services that could demonstrate expected loss of income due to their location in a COVID-19 hotspot, but it did not address the affordability costs for parents who may have lost income due to the pandemic. Overall, it was less generous and less well-equipped to address the cumulative impact of the pandemic crisis across the sector and its workforce, leaving the sector in an acute state of crisis.

Children's access to early learning was compromised through the pandemic, with one study reporting the number of children aged 0 to 12 years using approved child care services halved from 52 per cent early in 2020 to 26 per cent in May–June 2020 (Australian Institute of Family Studies 2021a, 2021b). Peak virus outbreaks also saw child care centres close. During the January 2022 Omicron crisis, 268 centres in New South Wales were registered as closed due to the high level of staff and children isolating or ill with COVID-19 (Australian Children's Education and Care Quality Authority 2022b).[8]

The need for the 2020 and 2021 emergency packages highlights the critical policy tension that lies at the centre of Australia's ECEC system: although ECEC is an essential public service, policy settings frame it as a commodity to be delivered primarily by the private sector. The tension between delivery of a public good and the private provision of services in which the only two revenue streams are the Commonwealth CCS (linked to enrolment numbers) and parent fees imposes a serious

---

7   See https://bit.ly/46Xbmdt.
8   This data is for Tuesday, 4 January 2022. Closures had reduced to almost half at 124 on 31 January.

and structural limitation on the funding of a universal high-quality service accessible to all children, delivered by a professionally trained and paid ECEC workforce.

4.5 Potential avenues for change

The disruption to families' work and care arrangements throughout the COVID-19 pandemic accentuated key gaps in policy settings and highlighted the difficulties parents face in reconciling work and care. Changes to patterns of work, including sustained periods of working from home, caused many families to rethink their preferred patterns of care and work. The devastating impact of the pandemic on families, formal ECEC services and workforce sustainability points to the urgent need for policy renewal and a system better calibrated to the needs of children, parents and ECEC workers. At this historic moment, there is an opportunity for policymakers to address the tensions that have troubled the ECEC sector for decades.

In the crisis context, policy ideas that political leaders had long declared impossible were suddenly implemented. For three short months, parents were given access to free child care – an idea previously rejected as unworkable by both major parties. Although it was not sustained, it did happen. Entrenched low pay for the ECEC workforce is also being addressed by some providers. In July 2021, Australia's largest not-for-profit early learning and care provider, Goodstart, increased the starting salaries of university-trained ECEC teachers to match those provided in the school sector – an increase of 10 per cent or more for most teachers. The wages of other trained educators were also raised 3 per cent – 5 per cent above the award rate for the sector.[9] Anecdotal evidence suggests some smaller providers are paying above award wages in recognition of the value of the work, and in order to retain highly skilled staff. While Australia's ECEC policy settings are far from optimal, these examples show it is possible for government and providers to make changes that support better work–care reconciliation

---

9   See https://bit.ly/48exCk5.

for parents, improve outcomes for children, and build sustainable jobs and careers for the ECEC workforce.

The pandemic experience has also sparked a new global conversation about the value of care, and there are widespread calls for new investment in care infrastructure, especially ECEC. While policies that support robust ECEC infrastructure and decent work–care reconciliation have long been the status quo in Nordic economies, such as Denmark, Finland and Sweden, similar policy settings in the wealthy Anglo neoliberal market economies of Australia, Canada, the United Kingdom and the United States have lagged. However, the COVID-19 recovery is driving change. In the United States, the Biden Administration included a bold policy agenda for early learning and care as a critical plank in the COVID-19 response.[10] This includes billions of dollars to improve child care affordability and deliver free pre-K education to all three- and four-year-olds as well as guaranteed access to high-quality, affordable child care for younger children from low- and middle-income families. In addition, the American Jobs Plan includes a US$25 billion Child Care Growth and Innovation Fund to improve the supply of child care by constructing new facilities and renovating existing child care facilities.[11] In Canada, the highlight of the Trudeau government's first COVID-19 budget was a C$30 billion investment in ECEC over five years with an additional C$9.2 billion every year after as a central plank in its COVID-19 recovery plan. This investment is designed to create a Canada-wide, community-based system of quality child care that will give parents access to C$10-per-day child care within five years (Department of Finance, Canada 2021). In collaboration with the provinces, the new Canadian national system prioritises public investment in the not-for-profit community sector as the best way to deliver stable provision of high-quality, affordable and inclusive early learning and care services that meet the needs of children and their families.[12] Importantly, new investment for the not-for-profit sector will rebalance the ECEC

---

10 Fact Sheet: How the Build Back Better Plan Will Create a Better Future for Young Americans. https://bit.ly/3TchE5N.
11 Fact Sheet: The American Jobs Plan. https://bit.ly/47L8uBW.
12 See https://bit.ly/3Gyz5pL.

system, reducing the market power of for-profit providers (Friendly et al. 2021; Kahn & Sterling 2021).

As noted above, investment in ECEC was a major issue in the May 2022 federal election and, for the first time, a major political party (Labor) described investment in ECEC as "essential family infrastructure" and "bold economic reform" (Rishworth 2021). This change in approach was largely driven by community recognition of the value of ECEC and an understanding that Australia cannot continue to undervalue this essential work or free-ride on the women who perform the majority of care for children, in either an unpaid or paid capacity. New investment in services that provide universal access to all children could be achieved in a variety of ways. Treating the early years as a critical investment in human capital in the same way as school education would deliver free public services to all in a way that would be transformative for children, families, the economy and society. Other more incremental changes to the existing child care subsidy system could achieve a similar outcome if work activity tests and caps on subsidies were removed and taper rates flattened (KPMG 2020; Wood et al. 2020). However, only new investment in the sector will lift wages to reflect the professional skills and expert work done by the ECEC workforce. This depends on government commitment to the educational role of ECEC, and the long-term benefits for young children. In addition, workplace policy settings that provide both men and women with adequate paid leave to care for children and family will also require increased investment (see Chapter 3 in this volume). In combination, these types of policy reforms will embed the right to care with decent work conditions, and the right for young children to be educated and cared for, into a new social contract between government and citizens.

Reform of the ECEC system is urgent, but there is no quick fix. While the federal Albanese government's goal of cheaper child care is welcome, it is not an adequate foundation for long-term policy development. Commitments to enhance and sustain the quality of ECEC provision are also essential, requiring evidence-based policy design and adequate funding. Prior to the initiation of the Productivity Commission inquiry, Labor's exclusive focus on the cost of ECEC ran the risk of losing sight of the multiple longer term benefits of investing in quality ECEC delivered by a well-trained and properly supported workforce. Adequate investment in early years learning and care will be costly, but as critical social infrastructure that drives wellbeing and productivity, it can no longer be overlooked. Given the system is currently at a breaking point, the policy response required must rely on long-term and sustained investment in policy renewal for workforce development and universal service provision. The National Children's Education and Care Workforce Strategy for 2022–2031 (Australian Children's Education and Care Quality Authority 2022b) reflects the need to build the future of ECEC in a careful and considered manner. The new strategy recognises the complexity of the workforce challenges that are needed to deliver sustainable high-quality services for all children and includes a collaborative plan involving all stakeholders (Education Services Australia 2022). The Productivity Commission inquiry is due to deliver its report into the delivery of "affordable, accessible, equitable and high-quality ECEC" in mid-2024. Policy reforms and inquiries of this type are important steps in the right direction.

References

Adamson, E., and Brennan, D. (2014). Social investment or private profit? diverging notions of "investment" in early childhood education and care. *International Journal of Early Childhood* 46(1), 47–61.

Australian Bureau of Statistics (2020). *Barriers and Incentives to Labour Force Participation 2018–19, Australia, August 2020*. Cat. No. 6238.0.55.001. https://bit.ly/486HcWl.

Australian Bureau of Statistics (2018). *Childhood Education and Care, June 2017*. Cat. No. 4402.0. https://bit.ly/3RHXgbT.

Australian Children's Education and Care Quality Authority (2022a). *NGF Snapshot Q2 2022*. https://bit.ly/41fVMsw.

Australian Children's Education and Care Quality Authority (2022b). Service and temporary closure information. https://bit.ly/41f5Ema.

Australian Children's Education and Care Quality Authority (2021a). *National Children's Education and Care Workforce Strategy, 2021, Workforce Snapshot*. https://snapshots.acecqa.gov.au/workforcedata/index.html.

Australian Children's Education and Care Quality Authority (2021b). *Shaping Our Future: A Ten-Year Strategy to Ensure a Sustainable, High-Quality Children's Education and Care Workforce 2022–2031.* https://bit.ly/46PBhnm.

Australian Children's Education and Care Quality Authority (2019). *Progressing a National Approach to the Children's Education and Care Workforce: Workforce Report November 2019.* https://bit.ly/3GA51tU.

Australian Institute of Family Studies (2021a). *Towards COVID normal: Employment and Work–Family Balance in 2020.* https://bit.ly/46K4Jet.

Australian Institute of Family Studies (2021b). *Families in Australia Survey: Towards COVID Normal. Report No. 3 Child Care in 2020.* https://bit.ly/46Uijfj.

Australian Treasury (2020). *Fact Sheet: Economic Response to the Coronavirus: JobKeeper Payment – Information for Employers.* https://bit.ly/3t9KzwS.

Berg, L. and Meagher, G. (2018). *Cultural Exchange or Cheap Housekeeper? Findings of a National Survey of Au Pairs in Australia.* Migrant Worker Justice Initiative. https://doi.org/10.13140/RG.2.2.17089.81769.

Centre for Policy Development (2021). *Starting Better: A Guarantee for Young Children and Families, November 2021.* https://bit.ly/481V6JT.

Chalmers, J (2023) Terms of Reference for Productivity Commission inquiry into the early childhood education and care (ECEC) sector in Australia, 9 February 2023, https://bit.ly/3RHXnEl.

Cloney, D., Cleveland, G., Hattie, J. and Tayler, C. (2016). Variations in the availability and quality of early childhood education and care by socioeconomic status of neighborhoods. *Early Education and Development* 27:3: 384–401. https://doi.org/10.1080/10409289.2015.1076674.

Cortis, N., Blaxland, M. and Charlesworth, S. (2021). *Challenges of Work, Family and Care for Australia's Retail, Online Retail, Warehousing and Fast Food Workers.* Sydney: Social Policy Research Centre, UNSW Sydney.

Dent, G. (2021). 73% of early educators plan to leave the sector within three years. *The Women's Agenda.* https://bit.ly/47MuYCw.

Department of Education (2021). *Child Care in Australia Report, June Quarter 2021.* https://bit.ly/47DQtFv.

Department of Education, Skills and Employment (2020). *Early Childhood Education and Care Relief Package: Four Week Review. Summary Report 18 May 2020.* https://nla.gov.au/nla.obj-2685365763/view.

Department of Finance, Canada (2021). Budget 2021: A Canada-wide Early Learning and Child Care Plan. Ottawa: Canadian Government. https://bit.ly/3Rf853l.

Eastman, C., Charlesworth, S. and Hill, E. (2018). *Fact Sheet 2: Child Carers.* https://bit.ly/3GwFamq.

Education Services Australia (2022). *Shaping Our Future: A Ten-Year Strategy to Ensure a Sustainable, High-Quality Children's Education and Care Workforce 2022-2031.* Licensed by the Education Ministers Meeting under a Creative Commons Attribution. https://bit.ly/3PFQh0I.

Emery, K. (2021). COVID keeps grandparents and international au pairs shut out of WA. *The West Australian*, 11 August. https://bit.ly/3PP3WCx.

Friendly, M., Vickerson, R., Mohamed, S., Rothman, L. and Nguyen, N.T. (2021). *Risky Business: Child Care Ownership in Canada Past, Present and Future, 30 June 2021, Occasional Paper 34.* Toronto, Canada: Childcare Resource and Research Unit.

The Front Project (2020). *Early Learning and COVID: Experiences of Teachers and Educators at the Start of the Pandemic.* https://bit.ly/3Ndpdpi.

The Front Project (2019). *A Smart Investment for a Smarter Australia: Economic Analysis of Universal Early Childhood Education in the Year Before School in Australia.* Melbourne: PricewaterhouseCoopers. https://bit.ly/3GBFVLf.

Gromada, A. and Richardson, D. (2021). *Where Do Rich Countries Stand on Childcare?* Florence: UNICEF Office of Research – Innocenti.

Hamilton, M., Hill, E. and Kintominas, A. (2021). Moral geographies of care across borders: the experience of migrant grandparents in Australia. *Social Politics: International Studies in Gender, State and Society.* https://doi.org/10.1093/sp/jxab024.

Hamilton, M. and Suthersan, B. (2020). Gendered moral rationalities in later life: older women balancing work and care of grandchildren in Australia. *Ageing and Society* 41(7): 1651–72.

Heckman, J.J. (2012). Invest in early childhood development: reduce deficits, strengthen the economy. *The Heckman Equation* 7: 1–2.

Hill, E. and Wade, M. (2018). "The radical marketisation" of early childhood education and care in Australia. In D. Cahill and P. Toner, eds. *Wrong Way: How Privatisation and Economic Reform Backfired*, 21–39. Carlton: La Trobe University Press in conjunction with Black Inc.

Howe, J., Charlesworth, S. and Brennan, D. (2019). Migration pathways for frontline care workers in Australia and New Zealand: front doors, side doors, back doors and trapdoors. *UNSW Law Journal* 42(1): 211–41.

Hurley, P., Matthews, H. and Pennicui, S. (2022). *Deserts and Oases: How Accessible is Childcare?* Mitchell Institute, Victoria University. https://bit.ly/484Dg8u.

id.community (2022). Community profiles, Australia: unpaid childcare. https://bit.ly/3Rx4aAi.

Jackson, J. (2020). *Every Educator Matters: Evidence for a New Early Childhood Workforce Strategy for Australia*. Melbourne: Mitchell Institute, Victoria University.

Kahn, S. and Sterling, S. (2021). *Supply-side Childcare Investments: Policies to Develop an Equitable and Stable Childcare Industry. Issue Brief*. New York: The Roosevelt Institute. https://bit.ly/3RR5Fdw.

King, D. and Meagher, G. eds (2009). *Paid Care in Australia: Politics, Profits, Practices*. Sydney: Sydney University Press.

Klapdor, M. (2020). COVID-19 Economic response—free child care. Parliamentary Library, FlagPost blog, 6 April. https://bit.ly/46Pw2nG.

KPMG (2020). *The Child Care Subsidy: Options for Increasing Support for Caregivers*. https://bit.ly/3RvMTaW.

Lucas, F. (2021). Three-year-old preschool trial begins in the Northern Territory. *The Sector*, 12 August. https://bit.ly/3Njf7D5.

McDonald, P., Thorpe, K. and Irvine, S. (2018). Low pay but still we stay: retention in early childhood education and care. *Journal of Industrial Relations* 60(5): 647–68.

New South Wales Government (2022). *The Early Years Commitment: A Brighter Future for NSW Families*. https://bit.ly/3TrfAHi.

Newberry, S. and Brennan, D. (2013). The marketisation of early childhood education and care (ECEC) in Australia: a structured response. *Financial Accountability and Management* 29(3): 227–45.

Noble, K. and Hurley, P. (2021). *Counting the Cost to Families: Assessing Childcare Affordability in Australia*. Victoria University. https://bit.ly/3RA8AGV.

OECD (2021). PF3.1: Public spending on childcare and early education. OECD Family Database, oe.cd/fdb, updated September 2021. https://bit.ly/46QCFq3.

OECD (2020). *Building a High-Quality Early Childhood Education and Care Workforce: Further Results From the Starting Strong Survey 2018*. Paris: TALIS, OECD Publishing. https://doi.org/10.1787/b90bba3d-en.

Oishi, N. and Ono, A. (2020). North–North migration of care workers: "Disposable" au pairs in Australia. *Journal of Ethnic and Migration Studies* 46(13): 2682–99.

The Parenthood (2021a). *Making Australia the Best Place in the World to be a Parent*. The Parenthood. https://bit.ly/46lunqJ.

The Parenthood (2021b). *Government Must Respect Early Educators*. https://www.theparenthood.org.au/early_educators_day.

Pascoe, S. and Brennan, D. (2017). *Lifting Our Game: Report of the Review to Achieve Educational Excellence in Australian Schools Through Early Childhood Interventions*. Melbourne: Government of Victoria.

Penn, H. (2011). Policy rationales for early childhood services. *International Journal of Child Care and Education Policy* 5(1): 1–16.

Pricewaterhouse Coopers (2019). *A Smart Investment for a Smarter Australia: Economic Analysis of Universal Early Childhood Education in the Year Before School in Australia.* https://bit.ly/3RfTBjO.

Prime Minister and Minister for Education (2020). Early Childhood Education and Care Relief Package, Joint media release, 2 April. https://bit.ly/46SYa9w

Productivity Commission (2022). *Report on Government Services 2022, Chapter 3: Early Childhood Education and Care.* Canberra: Australian Government.

Productivity Commission (2021). *Report on Government Services 2021, Chapter 3: Early Childhood Education and Care.* Canberra: Australian Government.

Rishworth, A. (2021). The economic case for increased investment in early learning and care. Virtual address to the McKell Institute, 8 November.

Rutter, J. and Evans, A. (2012). *Improving Our Understanding of Informal Childcare in the UK: An Interim Report of Daycare Trust Research into Informal Childcare.* London: The Daycare Trust.

SNAICC (2021). *Framework to Inform the Development of a National Aboriginal and Torres Strait Islander Early Childhood Strategy.* Secretariat of National Aboriginal and Islander Child Care. https://bit.ly/46NZIBB.

Stewart, M. (2021). *Tax and the Fertility Freefall: Children, Care and the Intergenerational Report.* Melbourne: Melbourne School of Government.

Sydenham, E. (2019). *Ensuring Equality for Aboriginal and Torres Strait Islander Children in the Early Years: Discussion Paper.* Melbourne: Secretariat of National Aboriginal and Islander Child Care.

Thorpe, K., Jansen, E., Sullivan, V., Irvine, S., McDonald, P. and Spall, E. (2020). Identifying predictors of retention and professional wellbeing of the early childhood education workforce in a time of change. *Journal of Educational Change* 21: 623–47.

Thrive By Five (2017). *Time to Act: Investing in Our Children and Our Future.* https://bit.ly/4a2MtzU.

United Workers Union (2021a). *Exhausted, Undervalued and Leaving: The Crisis in Early Education.* https://www.voced.edu.au/content/ngv%3A91207.

United Workers Union (2021b). *"Spitting Off Cash": Where Does All the Money Go in Australia's Early Learning Sector?* https://bit.ly/419qOIL.

Victorian Government (2022). Best Start, Best Life: Three-Year-Old Kindergarten for Victoria. https://www.vic.gov.au/three-year-old-kindergarten-victorians.

Whiteford, P., Redmond, G. and Adamson, E. (2011). Middle class welfare in Australia: How has the distribution of cash benefits changed since the 1980s? *Australian Journal of Labour Economics* 14(2): 81.

Wood, D., Griffiths, K. and Emslie, O. (2020). *Cheaper Childcare: A Practical Plan to Boost Female Workforce Participation* (Vol. 9). Melbourne: Grattan Institute. https://bit.ly/3uPInLq.

5

Flexible work policy: Building "good flex" across the life course

Rae Cooper, Frances Flanagan and Meraiah Foley

5.1 Introduction

Workplace flexibility, or "the ability of workers to make choices influencing when, where, and for how long they engage in work-related tasks" (Hill et al. 2008: 149), has been the subject of increasing attention from employment relations scholars and policymakers over the past decade. Having access to the right amount and the right type of workplace flexibility is critical for making work sustainable and "workable" for employees as they try to manage their responsibilities and commitments in paid employment alongside those of family and community. Yet, when we talk about flexible work, we are often speaking at cross-purposes.

For some observers, "flexible work" speaks to the agency of workers and their ability to craft work to meet their own needs. In this chapter, we call this "good flex". For others, flexible work denotes precarious and poorly rewarded work where the flexibility overwhelmingly benefits employers and workers have low levels of control over these arrangements. We call this "bad flex". As the COVID-19 pandemic disrupted global ways of working, we saw extreme examples of both "good" and "bad" flex in the labour market. On the one hand, many workers, especially professional and managerial employees, experienced their first opportunity to work remotely at home (Lee et al. 2022). Survey after survey shows that this experience led to a sharp rise in demand for hybrid working and "good flex" as employees imagine a post-COVID-19 future of work (Baird & Dinale 2020). This sharply contrasts with the flexibility experienced by frontline workers through the pandemic, especially those employed on insecure contracts in sectors like hospitality, accommodation and retail. Here workers experienced "bad flex" that resulted in severe loss of jobs and hours, with each wave of lockdown compounding their insecurity (Foley & Cooper 2021).

In this chapter, we argue that current policy settings in Australia provide weak incentives for "good" flexibility to flourish. Instead, "bad flex" – a one-sided, employer-oriented form of flexibility – remains the most common flexibility experience of Australian workers, particularly those in lower-paid occupations and industries, and is most often manifested in the form of casualised labour. We argue there is an urgent need for regulatory and organisational change to stop the spread of low-end flexibility like casual employment and to build access to high-quality flexible work. This is what is needed to support workers' capacity to combine regular care duties with good and rewarding work. We begin the chapter by discussing the policy context and meaning of flexible work in Australia, before turning to an examination of how the current policy architecture incentivises bad flex. Finally, we address the current tensions and debates on flexible work over the life course, and present potential avenues for change.

5.2 The meaning of workplace flexibility

To understand the policy history and context of flexible work in Australia, it is important to first recognise that all forms of workplace flexibility are not equal. Indeed, the concept of flexible work has multiple dimensions. The classic definitions of flexible work usually encompass temporal, spatial and contractual elements (Bessa & Tomlinson 2017). Temporal flexibility describes the hours of work, which might include flexibilities such as part-time working, job-sharing, staggered start and finish times, or school term-time working. Spatial flexibility refers to the place of work where flexibilities may include work being undertaken at home rather than in a workplace, or on a hybrid basis in a mix of workplace and remote settings. Contract flexibility refers to variations in the standard employment relationship of long hours and permanent working arrangements. Relevant examples include casual working, zero-hours contracts, short-term contracts or different types of "gig work".

In this chapter, we draw a simple distinction between "good" and "bad" forms of flexible work, concepts that broadly correlate with whether the flexibility in question is *worker*-oriented or *employer*-oriented (Rubery et al. 2016; Heron & Charlesworth 2012; Tilly 1996). "Mutually beneficial flexibility" (Tomlinson et al. 2018), or "good flex", allows workers to access the flexibility they need to meet their work and life commitments at different life stages and provides employers with skilled, stable and productive workforces. Good flex requires that workers have a degree of control and choice over the types of flexibility they access, coupled with the capacity to exercise voice, or "have a say", to signal needs and preferences. Good flex allows workers to construct and progress within careers, underpinned by secure employment and a living wage, rather than simply working in low-paid and precarious jobs. On the other hand, in bad flex work, the timing and duration of work is overwhelmingly controlled by the employer and oriented to the needs of the enterprise, with little scope for control or meaningful negotiation based on the needs of the employee. While good flex enables workers to negotiate their work and care commitments over the life course, bad flex offers, at best, a stopgap approach to managing these obligations and, at worst, represents a form of labour market exploitation (Bessa & Tomlinson 2017).

Bad flex is abundant in the Australian labour market, facilitated and incentivised by Australia's policy architecture and the inflexibility of many permanent jobs. It most commonly takes the form of casual employment but is also apparent in forms of dependent contracting and labour hire, and in platform-based work. This form of flexibility is strongly gendered. Women dominate in casual jobs, holding 53.8 per cent of casual employment in August 2021 (Australian Bureau of Statistics 2022a). This form of employment is often the only available option for women with care responsibilities, squeezed between inflexible, long-hours secure employment and an inadequate care regime with expensive and hard-to-access paid care and underdeveloped paid leave options (see Chapters 3 and 6 in this volume). Casual employment seems to have become a uniquely Australian "solution" to this clash and puts pressure on carers, especially mothers of young children. For women, it is those aged 15–34 years who are the most likely (36.3 per cent) to be employed casually. The (structured) choice of women to engage in low-quality precarious employment, like casual work, has consequences for their long-term economic security leading to low wages, underemployment, poor access to more lucrative jobs within organisational hierarchies and woefully inadequate retirement savings (Birch & Preston 2021).

5.3 Current policy architecture

The current policy architecture in Australia has three main forms of flexibility: casual working arrangements; the right to request flexible work arrangements and "individual flexibility arrangements" (IFAs) in the *Fair Work Act 2009* (Cth); and flexibility enshrined in awards. The limitations and poor design of these settings support bad flex work arrangements and offer few meaningful legal pathways for employees with bad flex to transition to good flex employment. This creates a two-track system where workers have either good or bad flex options available to them.

Casual employment

Casual employment is defined by the *Fair Work Act* as work where the offer of employment was made and accepted "on the basis that the employer makes no firm advance commitment to continuing and indefinite work according to an agreed pattern of work for the person" (s 15A(1)). In terms of the statistical definition for ABS statistics, casual employment is employment which does not have paid sick or annual leave. In November 2020, 22 per cent of all Australian employees were employed casually and nearly half (48 per cent) of part-time workers, the majority of whom are women, were not entitled to paid leave

(Australian Bureau of Statistics 2022b). Australia's density of casual employment has long been among the highest in the OECD (Tweedie 2013; Burgess et al. 2008) and makes up a particularly significant proportion of employment in essential industries such as disability services (42 per cent) (Macdonald & Charlesworth 2021), health care and social assistance generally (21.4 per cent), and in cleaning and laundry services (45 per cent). These industries are highly feminised, accentuating women's unequal status in the labour market. Casualisation rates in Australia have remained high and stable for approximately two decades (Markey & McIvor 2018).

Casual workers do not enjoy mainstream workplace conditions that, in part, provide critical care supports. Under the *Fair Work Act*, casual workers are excluded from accruing annual leave (s 86), paid personal/carers leave (s 95) and paid compassionate leave (s 106), exclusions which are notionally compensated in modern awards by a 25 per cent "loading" on top of the base wage. Casuals do have rights under the *Fair Work Act* to unpaid leaves, including two days unpaid personal/carers leave (pt 2–2, div 7, sub-div B) and compassionate leave (s 104). The National Employment Standards also provide casual employees with pathways to permanent employment. However, these rights are inherently weak, involving rights to *request* permanency only. They also only apply in circumstances where working arrangements are minimally casual to begin with; namely, where a casual has been employed on a regular and systematic basis for a sequence of periods of employment of at least 12 months and there is a reasonable expectation of continuing employment (s 66F). Casual employees who decide that a regular employment contract would suit them better may request conversion to permanent employment, but employers may refuse such requests on several grounds, including if accepting would require a significant adjustment to the employee's hours of work, the employee's position will cease to exist in the period of 12 months after granting the request or there will be significant changes in the days or times at which the employee's hours of work are required to be performed (s 66H). While government does not systematically collect data and report on outcomes of conversion applications, sectoral estimates suggest that success rates are extremely low (e.g., less than 1 per cent in higher education), owing to multiple challenges the system poses for applicants (see Bare et al. 2021).

The right to request flexible work arrangements

Australia first introduced a formal right to request flexible work in 2010 as part of the National Employment Standards. Eligible workers included employees who were the parents of preschoolers or children under 18 with a disability. The new legislation provided these workers with a right to *request* flexible working arrangements from their employer as part of the minimum "safety net" for all employees covered by the federal system. Employees covered by the new legislation included those who had completed at least 12 months of continuous service immediately before making the request (s 65(2)(a)). Requests could be for a range of modifications, including shorter working hours, compressed schedules and/or remote working (Cooper & Baird 2015). Requests needed to be in writing and to include precise details of the changes desired and the reasons for the request. In 2013 the legislation was expanded to include all carers, including parents or guardians of school-age or younger children, those with a disability, those 55 years and older, and those experiencing domestic violence or those caring for someone experiencing domestic violence (Pocock & Charlesworth 2017). The changed rules for eligibility reflected efforts to make the regulations more broadly "carer" focused compared to the initial right to request provisions introduced in 2010.

From 2010 until late 2022, this right remained a right to *request* only, and not *receive*, flexibility. Employers were not bound to grant requests, but they needed to respond within 21 days and could refuse on "reasonable business grounds", a broad concept which includes the fact that new working arrangements would be too costly for the employer (s 65(5A)). Inadequate knowledge about the right to request by workers and the lack of a robust appeal process meant that, since it became operational in 2010, the rate of uptake remained very low, especially for men (Cooper & Baird 2015; Skinner & Pocock 2014).

In December 2022, the right to request was extended and strengthened when federal Workplace Relations Minister Tony Burke secured the support of the national parliament for wide-ranging amendments to the *Fair Work Act*, including to the "right to request". The changes, which came into effect in June 2023 set out a stronger process for the consideration of requests for flexibility, including compelling employers to justify their decision-making in relation to assessing a request and granting employees the capacity to appeal to the Fair Work Commission if they are unhappy with their employer's refusal of a request. These changes and their impact on access will need to be keenly monitored as the new processes take shape.

Individual flexibility arrangements

Alongside the provisions of the *Fair Work Act*, formal flexibility may also be achieved through "individual flexibility arrangements" (IFAs). These are written agreements between an individual employee and employer which cannot leave the employee worse off overall in comparison to their existing entitlements (ss 144 and 202). As there is no central data base of individual flexibility arrangements, it is not clear how widespread they are or how beneficial they have been to workers. However, there have been some high-profile cases of individual flexibility arrangements being used unlawfully by employers, such as *Fair Work Ombudsman v Australian Shooting Academy Pty Ltd* [2011] FCA 1064, where an employer threatened to dismiss an employee if he did not sign an individual flexibility arrangement. This mechanism, like the right to request, includes no scope for employees to achieve flexible arrangements as a right. In the absence of substantive statutory rights to flexible work for permanent employees, the realisation of flexible working arrangements in practice has been found to be closely linked to firm-level characteristics (Fagan & Walthery 2011), industry and occupational characteristics (Pocock & Charlesworth 2017), and the ways in which individual line managers understand, interpret and implement policies (Cooper and Baird 2015).

In addition to the statutory provisions of the *Fair Work Act*, modern awards and determinations of the Fair Work Commission, which prescribe minimum wages and conditions covering workers in a particular occupation, are also important in regulating flexible work. In 2018, the Fair Work Commission inserted a clause into all modern awards requiring employers to take additional steps in considering flexibility requests, including the obligation to discuss the request with the employee before responding and to genuinely try to reach an agreement (Fair Work Commission 2018). Historically, industry-based awards provided a basis for ensuring that the overall employment relations system was flexibly adaptive to the needs of both employees and employers in particular industries. However, there are concerns that the present system is not performing this function, particularly for working-time arrangements in the social, community, home care and disability services industry. Until 2022, part-time employees in this industry had no minimum engagement time under the relevant award, a situation that was amended by the Fair Work Commission in 2021, when two-hour minimum engagements were introduced for part-time and casual employees in the disability services and home care streams, and three-hour minimum engagements for employees in the social and community services streams (Fair Work Commission 2021).

5.4 Current debates and tensions

The imperative to boost access to high-quality workplace flexibility has been championed by academics and policymakers, and by diversity, equality and inclusion advocates, for many years, primarily as a mechanism to drive higher labour force participation (and thus the economic security) of highly skilled women workers (see Cooper & Hill 2021). The pandemic has given added impetus to this, especially as many workers have had their first taste of remote and hybrid working throughout 2020 to 2022. In this section, we examine the current debates and tensions around access to high-quality flexible work over the life course. Research on the challenges of reconciling work and care has increasingly emphasised the importance of adopting a life course perspective to understand more precisely the problems that emerge across careers and the potential solutions to these issues (e.g., Tomlinson et al. 2018; Moen & Sweet 2004). This research has shown that different career points and life stages present distinct, yet overlapping, challenges faced by employees, specifically women (Baird & Heron 2020). Following Baird and Heron (2020), we structure our discussion around three career stages – training, entry and early career, mid-career, and later career to retirement – each of which coincides with different stages in family life and work and care needs. We acknowledge that these stages are arbitrary and that the care needs of many workers will play out in different ways and will sometimes cross multiple stages. This has been highlighted in public conversations about "the sandwich generation" who are caring simultaneously for young children and ageing parents. In the following section, we briefly overview research on the intersections of paid work and care at the different life stages, attempting to understand the needs of employees at each stage, the organisational challenges they face in accessing the flexibility they need, and the institutional drivers of these tensions.

Training, entry and early career

Young workers are rarely the focus of attention in analyses of flexible work and the life course. The training, entry and early career phases are perhaps most closely associated with the time of women's lives that most closely conforms to the "ideal" unencumbered male worker figure (Acker 2006). Although some 350,000 young Australians are carers (McDougall et al. 2018), analyses of the work–life needs of young workers have tended to be concerned not so much with "care", but rather the interaction of work with other "markers of passage" in early adulthood, such as leaving home, marriage and parenthood, which have been observed to be occurring in increasingly non-linear, blended, synchronic or deferred ways (Nilan et al. 2007). Transitions for young people between work and study have been widely recognised to be more complex than they once were (Cebulla & Whetton 2018). Only around 12 per cent of young people now follow a "traditional", quasi-linear school-to-work transition, with significant proportions of youth instead adhering to a "work and study to work pathway" (24 per cent), a "work, with and without study pathway" (15 per cent), a prolonged "not in the labour force pathway" (10 per cent) or, most significantly, a "churning with work pathway" (39 per cent) (Cebulla & Whetton 2018: 308). Individuals in this latter group spent most of their time in work, and only briefly alternated between other activities, such as study. Young women, on average, emerge from this complex landscape more educated than young men, with 72 per cent of women and 69 per cent of men aged 20–24 holding tertiary qualifications (Baird & Heron 2020). Levels of underemployment for workers aged 15–24 are high in Australia, with over 22 per cent underemployed in February 2021 (Australian Bureau of Statistics 2021). Young people who complete full-time education have been observed to search for almost five years before gaining full-time employment in their chosen occupation, and almost three years to find any full-time work (Skujins & Lim 2015).

Lack of access to full-time and permanent work matters for young people even if they do not have caring obligations. This is because the capacity of young people to access "good flex potential" work later in their lives is shaped by the nature and quality of their work and training at this earlier stage. There is an abundant literature about the long-term scarring impacts of insecure work, which indicates that such workers face higher unemployment risks, heightened risk of remaining trapped in casual employment, and wage penalties in the long-term (Goldin & Mitchell 2017; Mooi-Reci & Wooden 2017; Scherer 2009), detriments that are not compensated for by wage loadings (Tweedie 2013). Secure early earnings matter for workers because without them they cannot acquire economic assets, which are integral to having power and meaningful choice around work flexibility at later stages, most crucially, secure housing and growing superannuation balances. Being in precarious employment itself has also been found to shape family formation decisions, and the willingness and capacity of young Australians to assume care obligations for young children (Scherer 2009).

The fact that good flex and permanent work is positioned in the Australian labour market as something of an elusive prize, rather than a generalised norm, creates and widens work inequalities between young people in their early working lives. Young people with middle-class family backgrounds are able to access and "tread water" in high-prestige, low-security labour markets for longer (Morgan 2015), and accept unpaid internships in fields that could potentially lead to professional work with potential for good flex later in life. In 2016, a national survey found that 58 per cent of working-age adults under 30 had undertaken such unpaid internships (Stewart et al. 2021), despite the mixed evidence of whether they offer a bridge to employment

(McDonald et al. 2021). Young workers with family supports are also better placed to risk spending time and money and acquire debt for higher education, which has been shown in some Australian studies to be offering decreasing (although still significant) relative future economic benefits (Cebulla & Whetton 2018). Young people excluded from taking such risks due to an absence of family wealth are more likely to find themselves in bad flex employment at later life stages, in occupations with a high proportion of casual employment or with very shallow occupational ladders or career structures (Thompson 2020).

Mid-career: Balancing work and family

The mid-career stage, when workers are balancing paid work and raising children, is when we typically think about the most acute need for flexibility at work. Recent decades have seen a sharp increase in women's employment and labour force participation rates during their peak child-bearing and child-raising years, roughly from ages 24 to 49 (Baird & Heron 2020). The percentage of dual-earner couple households with children under 18 has risen steadily from 52 per cent in 1991 to 61 per cent in 2016, with a corresponding decrease in the share of households with a stay-at-home mother (Baxter 2019). The employment rate of partnered women with very young children (under the age of five) more than doubled between 1985 and 2019, from 30 per cent to 63 per cent (Warren et al. 2020).

Parents still use very different, and strongly gendered, arrangements to balance paid work and care. Most fathers in couple households (77 per cent) work full-time, a proportion that has barely changed over the past 25 years (Warren et al. 2020; Baxter 2019). Only 5 per cent of fathers in couple households work part-time, compared to 40 per cent of mothers in couple households (Australian Institute of Family Studies n.d.). Among sole-parent households, which are predominantly headed by women (79.3 per cent), mothers are significantly less likely to be employed than fathers and are more likely to work part-time (Australian Bureau of Statistics 2020; Warren et al. 2020). Although fathers in Australia are entitled to request flexible work arrangements to care for children, they rarely do in practice. The proportion of fathers working part-time has not changed much in the past 25 years and the relatively low uptake of part-time work among fathers in dual-earner households persists even when the mother works full-time (Baxter 2019).

Women also spend more time than men caring for children and performing other household work (Craig et al. 2010; Sayer 2005; Bianchi et al. 2000). Australian time-use data collected between 2002 and 2015 shows that fathers spent, on average, 46 hours per week in paid employment, 16 hours per week on housework and 13 hours per week on child care. Mothers, in contrast, spent 20 hours per week in paid work, 30 hours on household work and 27 hours per week on child care (Baxter 2023). The traditional male breadwinner model has been replaced by a "modified male breadwinner model", in which fathers usually engage in full-time employment and mothers work part-time while acting as primary caregivers to their children (Baxter 2013, 2015; Pocock 2005). During the mid-career life stage, fathers use modified schedules and remote working arrangements to provide care for their children while mothers reduce their working hours to accommodate their relatively larger share of unpaid caregiving responsibilities.

It is therefore clear that the use of flexible work in the mid-career years is strongly gendered, and so are the long-term economic consequences. While some women in professional and managerial jobs may be able to negotiate good flex arrangements, such as permanent part-time work, such arrangements are also associated with reduced mobility between jobs and career progression (Durbin & Tomlinson 2014). Research evidence also suggests that workers in professional and managerial roles face a range of challenges in accessing good flex, stemming from weak rights in minimum standards, organisational policies that make flexibility inaccessible, long hours and "presenteeist" industry norms, and managerial opposition to flexible working (Cooper et al. 2021; Foley & Cooper 2021; Kossek & Thompson 2016). Thus, for many mid-career women, a lack of good-quality flexible jobs pushes them toward more precarious forms of bad flex employment, such as casual work and self-employment, which offer women some degree of schedule control and temporal flexibility at the expense of job security, leave entitlements and the ability to accrue adequate superannuation (Foley et al. 2018).

Although it may be tempting to assume that these patterns (and outcomes) are a function of rational decisions made at the work–family nexus, this narrative obscures the powerful societal and regulatory forces shaping these choices. A key issue that affects this life stage is the limited " right to request" available under national employment law, as detailed above, and the inability of workers to appeal managerial decisions. As a result, access relies heavily on managerial discretion and is uneven and, again, highly gendered (Cooper & Baird 2015). In short, it appears that once women are mothers they construct their own flexibility by working part-time hours, with implications for their lifelong economic security. A range of other national policies structure workers at this life stage, particularly mothers, into bad flex. These include gender inequitable paid parental leave (see Chapter 3), the cost of early childhood care and education (see Chapter 4) and Australia's tax and transfer system (see Chapter 7), which push women toward part-time or casual and lower-paid work (Wood et al. 2020; Kitchen & Wardell-Johnson 2018; Stewart 2017; Baird & O'Brien 2015). Workers at this life stage also struggle to access paid leave and good flex to self-care and attend to their reproductive health concerns, for example, to seek medical attention for assisted fertility treatments or pregnancy loss (see Chapter 2).

Late career to retirement

Over the last 40 years, there has been a growing recognition of the social, psychological and economic benefits that can flow from gradual, rather than "cliff-edge" approaches to the cessation of paid employment for older workers (Duberley et al. 2014). Research into the hopes and experiences of older workers reveals a variety of conceptions of this life phase. For some, this stage of life holds the promise of "re-inventive contribution", and the possibility of focusing on making meaningful contributions to organisations, families and communities after years of "pragmatic endurance" in their child-bearing years. Success during this time hinges on levels of "recognition, respect and living integrated lives" (O'Neil & Bilimoria 2005: 184). Scholars have highlighted the significance of "career crafting", and workers' capacity to work in a way that supports their values and commitments outside paid employment

(Duberley, et al. 2014). Such commitments often include the provision of regular unpaid child care to grandchildren, an activity of society-wide significance given the limited affordability and accessibility of early childhood education and care, particularly for parents with unpredictable working hours (Hamilton & Suthersan 2021). What is clear in the roughly three decades since mandatory retirement ages were prohibited in Australia is that meaningful choice about the nature and extent of paid employment for older Australians hinges on far more than the existence of laws or policies that technically permit staged retirement. It depends, rather, on a matrix of factors, including accessibility of good flex work, superannuation levels, housing security, economic resources, family responsibilities and personal health (Patrickson & Ranzijn 2004).

Older workers with ongoing employment who wish to reduce their hours of work through formal "right to request" mechanisms face the same barriers of practical access as younger workers; namely, the lack of any enforceable legal entitlement to receive working-time adjustments, only the right to request. Older workers may also face higher practical barriers than other workers as a consequence of the persistence of age discrimination in the workplace (Australian Human Rights Commission 2021) and a reluctance to ask, with some older people expressing concern that requesting flexibility at work would put them "in a bad light" with their employer (Senate Economics References Committee 2016: 37). Reluctant or unsuccessful requesters who have family obligations or health limitations may be faced with the "choice" to retire completely if they can afford to, or alternatively to accept bad flex jobs if they cannot.

Single women over 60 are the lowest income earning household group in Australia, and the most likely to live in poverty (Birch & Preston 2021; Wilkins 2017). UK researchers have found that many older workers accept lower-level jobs to supplement inadequate retirement incomes and because they have limited employment prospects; thus, precarity is compounded by the combination of precarious jobs, precarious welfare states and precarious households (Lain et al. 2019). In addition, many older workers experience "ontological precarity" and worry about the long-term sustainability of their jobs in the face of limited sources of retirement income and, in some cases, precarious household circumstances (Lain et al. 2019). In Australia, economic pressures on older women to accept bad flex work are reinforced by the superannuation system, which structurally favours higher income earners who have worked full-time without breaks. Calculations of levels of superannuation required for Australians to retire are premised on the assumption that retirees own their own homes, which is not the case for many people, particularly women, whose working lives have included extensive bad flex employment earlier in their careers. The choice to taper paid employment around life needs is further limited by means- and asset-testing for the age pension.

5.5 Potential avenues for change

The experience of flexibility (in both its good and bad forms) in the pandemic has created an impetus for change. The availability of employment that is simultaneously non-standard in its timing and duration and sufficiently secure to support people to meet their care obligations, without loss of status or future standing, is integral to the achievement of a new social contract and a gender-equal society after the COVID-19 pandemic. Such work must not only be technically available, but abundant, routine and easily accessible to employees at every level of income and status regardless of gender. Without easily accessible good flex work, workplaces will continue to operate as engines for the reproduction of labour market inequalities, functionally penalising those who do not conform to the ideal (unencumbered) worker through comparatively reduced status and pay (Acker 2006). Flexibility is thus a concept that is integral to equality, but it needs handling with care, and with the constant accompanying question, 'flexibility *for whom?*' (Kossek & Lautsch 2018).

Whether workers have access to good flex or bad flex shapes their employment trajectories and choices over the life course. In this chapter, we have discussed some key characteristics of "good" and "bad" flexible work at each life stage. For young workers, a major theme is the preponderance of bad flex in the form of casual employment and the differential capacity of workers, depending on socio-economic background, to manage precarity while acquiring the skills and qualifications that might lead to good flex employment later in life. In mid-career, employees' requirements for good flex arrangements are often most acute as they seek to combine work with care for young and school-age children, but here employer discretion plays a major role in enabling practical access to leave and flexibility. In late career and retirement, a phase where many older women face ongoing care commitments, the inequalities of lack of access to good flex accumulated over the life course compound, leaving significant numbers of Australians, especially women, facing poverty and precarity in older age.

Addressing these issues requires a three-pronged approach. The first is to radically curtail the extent of precarious, bad flex work in the Australian labour market at every life stage and to restore a paradigm of casual employment that is confined to situations where work is genuinely intermittent, irregular, unpredictable or seasonal. Casual work is inherently hostile to employee-centred flexibility choices and, under current law and policy settings, offers no meaningful pathway for employees to access good flex arrangements. This approach would involve changing the definition of casual employment in the *Fair Work Act*, to anchor it in terms of the nature of the work involved, rather than as presently defined (s 15A) in terms of whether an employee has accepted an offer for a job from an employer knowing that there is no firm advance commitment to ongoing work with an agreed pattern of work. It would also require new and wider pathways from casual work to permanency.

Second, it is crucial that rights for people in ongoing employment to request flexibility are strengthened. This might be achieved through positive obligations on employers to reasonably accommodate requests for flexible working arrangements, combined with the removal of the requirement of 12 months continuous service for requesters, and a more explicit and narrow definition of the circumstances in which employers are able to refuse requests, which are anchored in the nature of the occupation and enterprise rather than solely in employers' commercial preferences. These rights should also be secured by procedural mechanisms that enable employees to easily, quickly and affordably appeal employer decisions on flexibility requests. We note that some of these ideas, like the right to appeal employer decisions and the introduction of appeal rights, were implemented in amendments to the *Fair Work Act* in 2022. The impact of these changes, which came into effect in June 2023, will need to be monitored to assess the extent to which they encourage access to good flexibility.

Third, it is crucial to consider how employment relations' regulation of flexibility intersects with the suite of adjacent policy areas that determine the availability of good flex in practice, including paid parental leave arrangements, early childhood care and education, and the interface of the tax and transfer system with part-time work, superannuation and pension eligibility. Ultimately, employment regulation and adjacent social policies should work in harmony to achieve an objective that will render the whole Australian economy and society fairer and more resilient: a labour market that supports everyone to combine paid employment with service to their communities and families without social penalty, regardless of their gender or age.

References

Acker, J. (2006). Inequality regimes: gender, class, and race in organizations. *Gender and Society* 20(4): 441–64. https://doi.org/10.1177/0891243206289499.

Australian Bureau of Statistics (2022a). *Casual Employment.* https://bit.ly/47KeB9n.

Australian Bureau of Statistics (2022b). *Labour Force Survey, July 2022.* https://bit.ly/3uNoipd.

Australian Bureau of Statistics (2021). *Labour Force Survey, February 2021.* https://bit.ly/3Ra4gg1.

Australian Bureau of Statistics (2020). *Labour Force Status of Families.* https://bit.ly/3uMCcIa.

Australian Human Rights Commission (2021). *What's Age Got To Do With It? A Snapshot of Ageism across the Australian Lifespan.* Sydney: Australian Human Rights Commission.

Baird, M. and Dinale, D. (2020). *Preferences for Flexible Working Arrangements: Before, During and After COVID-19.* A research report to the Fair Work Commission. https://bit.ly/474oQo9.

Baird, M. and Heron, A. (2020). The life cycle of women's employment in Australia and inequality markers. In R.D. Lansbury, A. Johnson and D. van den Broek, eds. *Contemporary Issues in Work and Organisations: Actors and Institutions*, 42–56. Abingdon, UK: Routledge.

Baird, M. and O'Brien, M. (2015). Dynamics of parental leave in Anglophone countries: the paradox of state expansion in the liberal welfare regimes. *Community, Work and Family* 18(2): 198–217.

Bare, E., Beard, J. and Tija, I. (2021). Unis offered as few as 1 in 100 casuals permanent status in 2021. Why aren't conversion rules working for these staff? *The Conversation*, 10 December. https://bit.ly/3RLmjuV.

Baxter, J. (2013). *Employment Characteristics and Transitions of Mothers in the Longitudinal Study of Australian Children (LSAC)* (Occasional Paper No. 50). Melbourne: Australian Institute of Family Studies.

Baxter, J. (2015). *Child Care and Early Childhood Education in Australia*. Melbourne: Australian Institute of Family Studies.

Baxter, J. (2019). *Fathers and Work: A Statistical Overview*. Australian Institute of Family Studies. https://bit.ly/3RgSQH8.

Baxter, J. (2023). *Employment patterns and trends for families with children*. Australian Institute of Family Studies. https://bit.ly/3GO7KjG.

Bessa, I. and Tomlinson, J. (2017). Established, accelerated and emergent themes in flexible work research. *Journal of Industrial Relations* 59(2): 153–69. https://doi.org/10.1177/0022185616671541.

Bianchi, S.M., Milkie, M.A., Sayer, L.C. and Robinson, J.P. (2000). Is anyone doing the housework? Trends in the gender division of household labor. *Social Forces* 79(1): 191–228. https://doi.org/10.2307/2675569.

Birch, E. and Preston, A. (2021). Women, COVID-19 and superannuation. *Australian Journal of Labour Economics* 24(2): 175–98.

Burgess, J., Campbell, I. and May, R. (2008). Pathways from casual employment to economic security: the Australian experience. *Social Indicators Research* 88(1): 161–78. https://doi.org/10.1007/s11205-007-9212-5.

Cebulla, A. and Whetton, S. (2018). All roads leading to Rome? the medium term outcomes of Australian youth's transition pathways from education. *Journal of Youth Studies* 21(3): 304–23. https://doi.org/10.1080/13676261.2017.1373754.

Cook, J., Threadgold, S., Farrugia, D. and Coffey, J. (2021). Youth, precarious work and the pandemic. *YOUNG* 29(4): 331–348. https://bit.ly/3Rc2vyW.

Cooper, R. and Baird, M. (2015). Bringing the "right to request" flexible working arrangements to life: from policies to practices. *Employee Relations* 37(5): 568–81. https://doi.org/10.1108/ER-07-2014-0085.

Cooper, R. and Hill, E. (2021). *Building Access to High Quality, Flexible Work.* Gender Equality in Working Life Research Initiative Insights Series. Sydney: University of Sydney. https://doi.org/10.25910/X7N1-SA46.

Cooper, R., Baird, M., Foley, M., Oxenbridge, S. (2021). Normative collusion in the industry ecosystem: explaining women's career pathways and outcomes in investment management. *Human Relations* 74(11): 1916–41.

Craig, L., Mullan, K. and Blaxland, M. (2010). Parenthood, policy and work-family time in Australia 1992–2006. *Work, Employment and Society* 24(1): 27–45. https://doi.org/10.1177/0950017009353778.

Duberley, J., Carmichael, F. and Szmigin, I. (2014). Exploring women's retirement: continuity, context and career transition: exploring women's retirement. *Gender, Work and Organization* 21(1): 71–90. https://bit.ly/3RloHH4.

Durbin, S. and Tomlinson, J. (2014). Female part-time managers: careers, mentors and role models. *Gender, Work and Organization* 21(4): 308–20. https://doi.org/10.1111/gwao.12038.

Fagan, C. and Walthery, P. (2011). Individual working-time adjustments between full-time and part-time working in European firms. *Social Politics: International Studies in Gender, State and Society* 18(2): 269–99. https://doi.org/10.1093/sp/jxr011.

Fair Work Commission (2021). FWCFB 2383. Four yearly review of modern awards – *Social Community Home Care and Disability Services Industry Award 2010* – substantive claims. https://bit.ly/3RbOJfF.

Fair Work Commission (2018). FWCFB 5753. *Family Friendly Working Arrangements.* https://bit.ly/3Gzd1ve.

Foley, M., Baird, M., Cooper, R. and Williamson, S. (2018). Is independence really an opportunity? The experience of entrepreneur-mothers. *Journal of Small Business and Enterprise Development* 25(2): 313–29.

Foley, M. and Cooper, R. (2021). Workplace gender equality in the post-pandemic era: where to next? *Journal of Industrial Relations* 63(4): 463–76. https://doi.org/doi:10.1177/00221856211035173.

Goldin, C. and Mitchell, J. (2017). The new life cycle of women's employment: disappearing humps, sagging middles, expanding tops. *Journal of Economic Perspectives* 31(1): 161–82. https://doi.org/10.1257/jep.31.1.161.

Hamilton, M. and Suthersan, B. (2021). Gendered moral rationalities in later life: grandparents balancing paid work and care of grandchildren in Australia. *Ageing and Society* 41(7): 1651–72. https://bit.ly/3TfWfc1.

Heron, A. and Charlesworth, S. (2012). Working time and managing care under Labor: whose flexibility? *Australian Bulletin of Labour* 38(3). https://bit.ly/3RA3Px3.

Hill, J.G., Grzywacz, S.A., Blanchard V, Matz-Costa, C., Shulkin, S. and Pitt-Catsouphes, M. (2008). Defining and conceptualizing workplace flexibility. *Community, Work and Family* 11(2): 149–63. https://bit.ly/3t78hK6.

Kitchen, A. and Wardell-Johnson, G. (2018). *The Cost of Coming Back: Achieving a Better Deal for Working Mothers.* KPMG. https://bit.ly/3GyLCJN.

Kossek, E.E. and Lautsch, B.A. (2018). Work-life flexibility for whom? Occupational status and work-life inequality in upper, middle, and lower level jobs. *Academy of Management Annals* 12(1): 5–36. doi.org/10.5465/annals.2016.0059.

Kossek, E.E. and Thompson, R.J. (2016). Workplace flexibility: integrating employer and employee perspectives to close the research-practice implementation gap. In Tammy D. Allen and Lillian T. Eby, eds. *The Oxford Handbook of Work and Family*, 255–70. New York: Oxford University Press.

Lain, D., Airey, L., Loretto, W. and Vickerstaff, S. (2019). Understanding older worker precarity: the intersecting domains of jobs, households and the welfare state. *Ageing and Society* 39(10): 2219–41. https://bit.ly/484DNau.

Lee, T., Good, L., Lipton, B. and Cooper, R. (2022). Women, work and industrial relations. *Journal of Industrial Relations* 64(3): 347–61. https://doi.org/10.1177/00221856221099624.

Macdonald, F. and Charlesworth, S. (2021). Regulating for gender-equitable decent work in social and community services: bringing the state back in. *Journal of Industrial Relations* 63(4). https://bit.ly/3RbOMrR.

Markey, R. and McIvor, J. (2018). Regulating casual employment in Australia. *Journal of Industrial Relations* 60(5): 593–618.

McDonald, P., Stewart, A. and Oliver, D. (2021). Challenging the assumptions supporting work experience as a pathway to employment. In A. Stewart, R. Owens, N. O'Higgins and A. Hewitt, eds. *Internships, Employability and the Search for Decent Work Experience*, 76–90. ILO Future of Work Series. International Labour Organization. Geneva: Edward Elgar Publishing.

McDougall, E., O'Connor, M. and Howell, J. (2018). "Something that happens at home and stays at home": an exploration of the lived experience of young carers in Western Australia. *Health and Social Care in the Community* 26(4): 572–80. https://doi.org/10.1111/hsc.12547.

Moen, P and Sweet, S. (2004) From "work–family" to "flexible careers", *Community, Work and Family* 7(2): 209–26. https://bit.ly/3R5nYt6.

Mooi-Reci, I. and Wooden, M. (2017). Casual employment and long-term wage outcomes. *Human Relations* 70(9): 1064–90. https://bit.ly/3NeMUgM.

Morgan, G. (2015). Youth and precarious work. *Social Alternatives* 34(4): 3–4.

Nilan, P., Julian, R. and Germov, J. (2007). *Australian Youth: Social and Cultural Issues*. Sydney: Pearson Education Australia.

O'Neil, D.A. and Bilimoria, D. (2005). Women's career development phases: idealism, endurance, and reinvention. *Career Development International* 10(3): 168–89. https://doi.org/10.1108/13620430510598300.

Patrickson, M. and Ranzijn, R. (2004). Bounded choices in work and retirement in Australia. *Employee Relations* 26(4): 422–32. https://bit.ly/4aecn3J.

Pocock, B. (2005). Work/care regimes: institutions, culture and behaviour and the Australian case. *Gender, Work and Organization* 12(1): 32–49. https://bit.ly/3Gwdrmb.

Pocock, B. and Charlesworth, S. (2017). Multilevel work–family interventions: creating good-quality employment over the life course. *Work and Occupations* 44(1): 23–46. https://doi.org/10.1177/0730888415619218.

Rubery, J., Keizer, A. and Grimshaw, D. (2016). Flexibility bites back: the multiple and hidden costs of flexible employment policies. *Human Resource Management Journal* 26(3): 235–51. https://bit.ly/3Nj1tjg.

Sayer, L.C. (2005). Gender, time and inequality: trends in women's and men's paid work, unpaid work and free time. *Social Forces* 84(1): 285–303.

Scherer, S. (2009). The social consequences of insecure jobs. *Social Indicators Research* 93(3): 527–47. https://doi.org/10.1007/s11205-008-9431-4.

Senate Economics References Committee. (2016). *"A Husband Is Not a Retirement Plan": Achieving Economic Security for Women in Retirement*. Canberra: Parliament of Australia. https://apo.org.au/node/187691.

Skinner, N. and Pocock, B. (2014). *The Persistent Challenge: Living, Working and Caring in Australia in 2014*. Centre for Work + Life, University of South Australia. https://bit.ly/3Njg0eT.

Skujins, P. and Lim, P. (2015). *How Young People are Faring in the Transition from School to Work*. Melbourne: Foundation for Young Australians. https://apo.org.au/node/58442.

Stewart, A., Owens, R., O'Higgins, N. and Hewitt, A. (2021). Internships: a policy and regulatory challenge. In A. Stewart, R. Owens, N. O'Higgins and A. Hewitt, eds. *Internships, Employability and the Search for Decent Work Experience*, 2–16. ILO Future of Work Series. International Labour Organization. Geneva: Edward Elgar Publishing.

Stewart, M. (2017). *Tax, Social Policy and Gender*. Canberra: ANU Press. https://doi.org/10.22459/TSPG.11.2017.

Thompson, S. (2020). A vocational stream for social care workers: a case study. *Australian Journal of Adult Learning* 60(1): 22–43.

Tilly, C. (1996). *Half a Job: Bad and Good Part-time Jobs in a Changing Labor Market*. Philadelphia: Temple University Press.

Tomlinson, J., Baird, M., Berg, P., and Cooper, R. (2018). Flexible careers across the life course: advancing theory, research and practice. *Human Relations* 71(1): 4–22.

Tweedie, D. (2013). Precarious work and Australian labour norms. *The Economic and Labour Relations Review* 24(3): 297–315. https://bit.ly/4aaVVBd.

Warren, D., Lixia, Q. and Baxter, J. (2020). *Australian Families Then and Now: How We Worked*. Australian Institute of Family Studies. https://bit.ly/3Ry17rI.

Wilkins, R. (2017). *The Household, Income and Labour Dynamics in Australia Survey: Selected Findings from Waves 1 to 15*. Mlebourne: Melbourne Institute: Applied Economic and Social Research, The University of Melbourne.

Wood, D., Griffiths, K., Emslie, O. (2020). *Cheaper Childcare: A Practical Plan to Boost Female Workforce Participation*. Melbourne: Grattan Institute. https://bit.ly/3uPInLq.

6

Informal care policy: Needs of older people and people with disability or chronic illness

Myra Hamilton, Sara Charlesworth and Fiona Macdonald

6.1 Introduction

Aged and disability care services have made regular front-page news since 2020 as two Royal Commissions and the COVID-19 pandemic highlighted systems in crisis and systemic policy failure (Clun 2022; Campanella & Edmonds 2021; Henriques-Gomes 2020). However, the majority of care for older people and support for people with disability is not provided as formal care by specialist organisations but by informal carers, mostly family members in the home and community. In 2018, approximately one in 10 Australians (2.46 million people) were providing informal care for a person with a disability, chronic illness or frailty due to old age (Australian Bureau of Statistics 2018). Most of this care is provided by women, who are two and a half times more likely than men to be *primary* carers (Australian Bureau of Statistics 2018). A primary carer is defined as someone who provides the *most* informal assistance in their family to a person with disability, chronic illness or frailty due to old age.

Many informal carers rely in part on formal care services provided in the community and home through individualised-funding or consumer-directed care service models. The policy shift to care in the home has improved recognition of the rights and autonomy of older people and people with disability. However, it has also contributed to the increasing "familialisation" (see Eggers et al. 2020: 876) of care in Australia, whereby responsibility for managing the care and support of older people and people with disability is placed on the person themselves and their families. Thus, while disability and aged care services remain subsidised by the state, they are simultaneously heavily embedded in, and dependent upon, unpaid family labour to fill gaps in formal services and to organise and monitor formal service provision. The provision of unpaid familial care, no matter how desirable, is time consuming and often onerous, and places significant limitations on informal carers' opportunities for education, paid work, health, wellbeing and financial security (Constantin et al. 2022; Australian Human Rights Commission 2013b). This is not acknowledged in the current policy architecture for work and care in Australia, and services for carers are poorly integrated into the services available for older people and people with disability.

International research suggests that as the degree of familialisation increases, so too does the level of gender inequality in the distribution of those care responsibilities (Eggers et al. 2020). Indeed, the gendered impacts of care on labour market participation in Australia are stark and a key driver of economic insecurity and low retirement incomes for women (Jefferson 2009) with informal carers, particularly primary carers, reporting much lower levels of financial wellbeing than non-carers (University of Canberra and NATSEM 2021). In 2018, fewer than 53 per cent of male and 56 per cent of female primary carers were employed, compared with more than 81 per cent of male and 73 per cent of female non-carers. Participation in *full-time* work is even lower – only 20 per cent of female primary carers and less than 27 per cent of male primary carers were engaged in full-time employment across age groups (Australian Bureau of Statistics 2018). Without major reform to aged care and disability support systems to create more accessible, affordable and high-quality services, and much better support for family carers, informal carers in Australia are at high risk of sustained economic insecurity, poor health and low levels of wellbeing.

In this chapter, we first discuss the history of informal care for older people and people with disability or chronic illness. Then we examine the policy architecture of aged care in Australia, then disability care and support services. The chapter concludes with a discussion of the current policy tensions and debates and potential avenues for change.

6.2 History and context of aged care, disability support and informal carer services in Australia

In Australia over the last 40 years, there has been a move away from residential care towards care in the community and family. This shift recognises the benefits of community settings in meeting the needs and preferences of older people and people with disability (Oliver et al. 2020; Sixsmith & Sixsmith 2008). Today, approximately 66 per cent of disability care and support and 79 per cent of aged care support is provided outside of residential care settings (Department of Social Services 2021; Australian Institute of Health and Welfare 2020). Until the end of the 20th century, public funding for aged care and disability support services was predominantly in the form of block-funding to community-based services (or large government grants to approved providers to deliver services or programs) and funding for places in residential aged care facilities (Macdonald 2021; Fine & Davidson 2018). However, from the 1990s, changes to regulations and subsidy arrangements transformed the business models under which care services operated, creating competitive markets in which care providers were forced to tender for funding. This change allowed for-profit operators to enter care markets (Meagher 2021; Fine & Davidson 2018). At the same time, there was an increasing reliance on a "user-pays" model, particularly in aged care (Meagher 2021).

More recently, in both disability support and aged care, government policy has moved towards individualised or consumer-directed care models that focus on the preferences and autonomy of individual care "consumers" and allocate individual funding packages based on the level of assessed need (Hamilton et al. 2016; Needham 2011). Governments have withdrawn from directly paying providers to supply services, and now allocate funding to individuals to purchase their care on their own behalf in a competitive market (Meagher 2021; Brennan et al. 2017; Hamilton et al. 2016). This has been most clearly visible in the introduction of Home Care

Packages in community-based aged care settings, and in the introduction in 2013 of the National Disability Insurance Scheme, known as NDIS (Carer Respite Alliance 2021). The shift to marketised *consumer*-directed care has resulted in a systematic "de-prioritisation" of the needs of informal carers, a large majority of whom do not have their own needs met by available services (Carer Respite Alliance 2021: 10; Deloitte Access Economics 2020). The current lack of informal carer visibility and recognition in policy has become a significant challenge.

In Australia, public recognition of the role of informal carers first emerged in the 1990s, eventually resulting in the introduction of carer recognition legislation, first in most states and then at the Commonwealth level in 2010, such as the *Carers (Recognition) Act 2010* in New South Wales and the *Carer Recognition Act 2010* (Cth). Prior to this, policy and service contexts assumed that meeting the needs of older people and people with disability would, by implication, meet the needs of their informal carers. The legislative recognition of carers challenged this assumption and acknowledged that carers have their own independent needs that cannot be met simply through services for the care recipient. This change in approach saw the evolution of services focused on the specific needs of carers, such as the National Respite for Carers Program that provided information, advice, referral and respite to carers (Hamilton et al. 2016). Between 1996 and 2015, the National Respite for Carers Program was the largest program providing services directly to carers, with many carers also receiving services through state-based aged care and disability support programs. However, the introduction of the National Disability Insurance Scheme in 2013, and the Commonwealth Home Support Programme in aged care in 2015, saw a major reconfiguration of disability and aged care services in Australia that in turn marginalised carers' needs and saw the National Respite for Carers Program and other carer services become more difficult to access. These changes and the current policy architecture for aged and disability care services are set out below.

6.3 Current policy architecture

Aged care services

The current architecture of the aged care system in Australia is the result of various policy shifts since the late 1980s towards community-based services, marketisation, privatisation, home-based care and individualisation (Royal Commission into Aged Care Quality and Safety 2021). It is a system that relies heavily on informal care by family or others.

In residential aged care, care places are funded through subsidies from the Commonwealth government to providers. A growing proportion of services are delivered by very large for-profit providers, which currently provide 41 per cent of places, and this is growing (Aged Care Financing Authority 2021). The declining quality of care provided in residential aged care has been a growing concern over the last two decades with a rapid decrease in the proportion of nursing-qualified staff in the residential aged care workforce and a declining ratio of staff to residents (Eagar et al. 2019; Meagher et al. 2019). Poor-quality services can lead to greater stress experienced by informal carers and greater involvement of informal carers in advocacy, service navigation and direct care of family in residential aged care. For some families, this leads to them withdrawing their loved ones from residential aged care facilities (Royal Commission into Aged Care Quality and Safety 2021).

In the home care sector, there are two main programs: the Commonwealth Home Support Programme and the Home Care Packages Program. The Commonwealth Home Support Programme (CHSP), the largest program, remains block-funded, with the federal government directly funding providers based on client numbers and services delivered. It is mainly delivered by non-profit providers and is supposed to provide "entry level" services or low-level care and support activities such as meal support, home modifications and gardening assistance, social support and low-level personal care. The Home Care Packages Program (HCPP) was introduced in 2017 for individuals at four levels of assessed need, with Levels 1 and 2 providing lower levels of care and Levels 3 and 4 providing more intensive care and support in the areas of nursing and domestic assistance, social support, home modifications and mobility aids, daily essential activities or assistive technology. Informal carers, likely to be daughters, are often responsible for the organisation and monitoring of care provided under the Home Care Packages Program, but there is some evidence that the program's focus on the individual consumer has led to the needs of carers being overlooked (Skatssoon 2019). The time- and task-oriented allocation of, and charging for, care services under the Home Care Packages Program has fragmented working-time conditions for home care workers (Meagher et al. 2019), which directly affects the quality and continuity of services for both clients and their carers.

The promise of responsive personalised care in the Home Care Packages Program has proved illusory, with the Royal Commission into Aged Care Quality and Safety drawing attention to a number of systemic failures. These include long wait lists first for assessment and then for services, even when allocated, which has left many older people without any access to formal care; insufficient package funding to meet the care needs of recipients; and the decline of total care hours provided across all Home Care Packages Program levels despite the increasing frailty and high rates of co-morbidities among customers (Royal Commission into Aged Care Quality and Safety 2021). These deficits in the aged care system have a direct impact on informal carers because it makes it hard for them to take a break from their caring roles, engage in paid employment or look after their own health needs (Skatssoon 2019).

In theory, respite care is provided under both programs. However, for those in the Home Care Packages Program, respite care must be paid out of limited package funds, which heavily constrains the use of respite care by carers. Other impediments to respite care include the aged care system requirement that an informal carer self-identifies as a "carer" and knows how to access support; that many older people and their carers do not receive good-quality respite care when they need it; and that respite care is insufficiently flexible or available to meet the needs of older people and their carers (Royal Commission into Aged Care Quality and Safety 2021: 66).

Disability care and support services

Australia's National Disability Insurance Scheme (NDIS), phased in from 2013, established a needs-based system of care for people with disability, aged between nine and 65 that provides individualised support for approximately 500,000 people across Australia. In what was a major policy change and shake-up of existing arrangements, the national scheme replaced most of the disability (and carer) services that had previously been provided by states and territories under the National Disability Agreement.

The NDIS is based on a "cash-for-care" model that provides funds directly to eligible people for their care and support, rather than allocating funds to service providers. Importantly, the NDIS was not designed to supplement informal care but to provide adequate funding for the purchase of *formal* support and care services. This is significant because cash-for-care schemes that are most likely to support familialisation are those that provide only a low-level benefit or subsidy to supplement informal care or compensate informal carers. Further, unlike some international schemes, the NDIS rules also do not allow resident family members to be employed as paid carers (Da Roit & Moreno-Fuentes 2019; National Disability Insurance Agency n.d.). Planning for the NDIS proposed that the scheme could include provision for assessment of carers' needs and supports, although this was not included in the final design (Productivity Commission 2011, vol 1: 105, 313).

Ultimately, both system design and implementation factors have limited the capacity of the NDIS to support carers. Eligibility for NDIS-funded support is limited to people with "permanent and significant" disability, with assessment of need based on level of impairment (National Disability Insurance Agency 2019). There are an estimated 2.5 million people aged under 65 years with a disability who do not receive any support through the NDIS (Australian Bureau of Statistics 2018). Most of these people are likely to be considered ineligible based on level of impairment and they must rely on informal carers and/or access to mainstream services (Tune 2019). Other people with disability who do not receive assistance through the NDIS are people over 65 years and individuals and carers from vulnerable groups who do not "engage" with the NDIS to the same extent: Aboriginal and

Torres Strait Islander peoples, people from culturally and linguistically diverse communities, and people with psycho-social disabilities (Tune 2019: 81). People with higher incomes and education levels are more likely than others to get their support needs met through the NDIS (Malbon, Carey & Meltzer 2019; Warr et al. 2017).

The administrative complexity of the NDIS is another factor affecting both access to and utilisation of support funding. However, more generally, the personalised scheme places significant additional demands on the time and energy of carers and people with disability to manage their funded supports. Prior to the introduction of individualised funding, a service provider might co-ordinate and organise a person's support and care including, for example, managing all support and care workers, arranging activities, organising transport and adapting services to changing needs. Under individualised funding arrangements, however, all of these tasks plus management of payments can fall to individuals and their carers. Only a minority of people with disability have provision in their funded NDIS support to pay a service to co-ordinate their supports (Tune 2019).

When determining the types of supports that will be funded by the NDIS, the National Disability Insurance Agency is required to take into account what is "reasonable" to expect families, carers, informal networks and the community to provide. NDIS-funded support plans for people with disability can include all kinds of services and supports to assist people with activities of daily living and with building their independence and skills. However, a support plan can only include respite care where it is considered reasonable and necessary for that individual with disability. As noted above, there is no provision for respite care to be provided on the basis of a family carer's needs.

A 2019 review of the NDIS identified "an overreliance on the informal supports (carers) provide" (Tune 2019: 89). This review argued for the NDIS to fund supports to assist carers in maintaining their caregiving roles and to build the capacity and capability of families and carers as caregivers (Tune 2019: 103). Such supports might include, for example, counselling or education for carers on particular aspects of disability, or substitute services enabling carers to take time out. However, even this concern with carers is limited to an interest in their capacity to *maintain* caregiving and ameliorating the risk of their withdrawal from caring. Policy concern is not about carer wellbeing, their needs or aspirations, including participating in employment and reconciling work and care. Carers need supports that address their needs and opportunities for participation, independence and inclusion, not just as carers but as individuals in their own right.

Carer services and income support

The introduction of individualised funding in disability services and consumer-directed care in aged care limits opportunities for carers to access essential services such as respite. These constraints were exacerbated when a number of carer-specific services were subsumed into the new disability and aged care systems. For example, the National Respite for Carers Program, the most important program providing respite and other services directly to carers, was rolled into the Commonwealth Home Support Programme, discussed above, which meant that only carers of a person aged 65 and over and using the Commonwealth Home Support Programme could access these services. This excluded carers of people aged under 65, carers of people with high care needs, and carers whose care recipient cannot access the Commonwealth Home Support Programme. This marginalised pathways for carers to access support services that met their own health and wellbeing, training and employment and social needs (Temple & Dow 2018), including services that supported them to reconcile work and care, such as respite.

In 2019 and 2020, in recognition of this gap, the federal government designed and implemented a suite of services for carers available through a single online portal called the Carer Gateway. The Carer Gateway provides referral services, online support services such as information, counselling, peer support and coaching (i.e., goal-setting and planning) to support carers with their caring role, and in-person carer support services provided by 10 government-commissioned service providers around Australia (Carer Respite Alliance 2021). Some carers who meet eligibility requirements can access Carer Directed Support, or personalised support, in one of two forms: as one-off practical support with the cost of an item (e.g., equipment, educational course, etc.) that supports the carer in their caring role or with their education or employment; or as a Carer Directed Support Package, which includes a range of practical support over a 12-month period including respite, support with household maintenance or transport, to the (low) value of AU$1500–$3000 (Broady & Weber 2021). To date, data on the take-up and impact of Carer Directed Support is limited, but there is little scope within these services for meeting carers' work–care reconciliation needs.

In addition to support services, there are several income support payments made available by the federal government for informal carers of a person with a disability, chronic illness or frailty due to old age. For example, the Carer Payment is available to carers who provide ongoing and constant care for a person with a disability, chronic illness or frailty due to old age, provided they meet income and assets tests and both they and the person they care for are Australian citizens or permanent residents.[1] Recipients of a Carer Payment are entitled to work or study up to 25 hours a week (including travel time). However, research suggests that the 25-hour limit on work and study restricts carers' opportunities for participation in paid work and fails to accommodate diverse and changing care commitments among carers (Australian Human Rights Commission 2013b). There is also a Carer Allowance, a (low) supplementary payment provided to people who provide daily care to a person with a disability, illness or frailty due to old age. It is subject to residency requirements and has a higher means test than the Carer Payment.

Workplace provisions

The workplace is a critical domain for assisting in the reconciliation of work and care responsibilities (Perlow & Kelly 2014). As a result, government policy intervention for effective workplace policies is important to support worker-carers of older adults and people with disability. In 1990, Australia ratified ILO Convention No. 156 on

---

1   For the Carer Payment, the maximum fortnightly rate for a single is $971.50, just over half of the national minimum wage (it can be accompanied by other supplementary payments or concessions). Carer Allowance is much lower, at $144.80 per fortnight. These amounts are correct for September 2023.

Workers with Family Responsibilities, which underpinned a new legislative and policy framework supporting worker-carers at both the state/territory and federal levels. The framework includes specific provisions in both employment and anti-discrimination regulation that have been expanded and strengthened over time (Charlesworth & Elder 2012). Political discourse around work and family was initially narrowly conceived as flexibility for working mothers (Pocock & Charlesworth 2017), but this is slowly changing as the population ages and informal care demands on the workforce increase.

Following a 1995 test case brought by the Australian Council of Trade Unions, carers leave entitlements were introduced in industrial awards, which allowed eligible carers to access up to five days accumulated sick leave for family leave purposes. These entitlements were then folded into "personal/carers leave" in the National Employment Standards of the *Fair Work Act 2009* (Cth) and now provide up to 10 days leave. However, like all of the national employment standards, access to *paid* leave, including to annual leave, is not available to casual employees or to workers who are not employees (Campbell & Charlesworth 2020), although employees, including casuals, are entitled to two days *unpaid* carers leave each time an immediate family or household member needs care and support. Another relevant national employment standard for carers, the right to request flexible work arrangements, has proved a very limited "right" (see Chapter 5). Initially it applied only to parents with preschool children and children under 18 with a disability, but now covers all carers. However, only employees with at least 12 months continuous service and long-term casuals who have a reasonable expectation of continuing "regular and systematic" employment are eligible. Until very recently, unlike most of the other national employment standards, there was no right to any substantive appeal of an employer's decision to refuse a request (Campbell & Charlesworth 2020). However, reforms introduced in the *Fair Work Legislation Amendment (Secure Jobs, Better Pay) Act 2022* (Cth) have now extended appeal rights to these right to request provisions. Nevertheless, research suggests there is relatively poor awareness of the right to request among employees and employers and any additional flexibility negotiated by individual employees in most Australian workplaces remains dependent on individual supervisors (Pocock & Charlesworth 2017; Cooper & Baird 2015).

Regulation prohibiting discrimination against workers on the grounds of care responsibilities in state/territory and federal anti-discrimination laws has proved particularly ineffective despite the promise of more innovative provisions in some states that impose a positive duty on employers to accommodate workers' care responsibilities (Chapman 2018). However, such "duties to accommodate" are a long way from enshrining a *right* to care. In practice, anti-discrimination regulation requires individual workers to pursue any breaches of their rights. Any positive outcomes in conciliation, or in the very few cases that result in successful tribunal and court decisions, are restricted to remedying the harm done to the claimant rather than systemic changes in the workplace (Charlesworth 2011).

Elder and disability carers face different pressures from parents in the duration and intensity of caring responsibilities and require different workplace responses to support the effective reconciliation of work and care (Pocock & Charlesworth 2017). In Australia, there has been a growth in larger employers providing most carers with some formal access to flexibility (Workplace Gender Equality Agency 2019). However, the implementation of such policies has arguably been more focused on providing support to parents with young children, particularly mothers, rather than to carers for older adults and people with disability. These carers are much less likely than parents to ask for flexibility from their employers, although female carers are almost twice as likely than male carers to do so (Skinner & Pocock 2014: 4). Yet, those with other caring responsibilities experience equivalent levels of work–life interference to those with child care responsibilities (Skinner & Pocock 2014: 40).

6.4 Current policy tensions and debates

Recent policy changes in the areas of disability and aged care have created the conditions under which informal carers are under intensified pressure to undertake care responsibilities and navigate complex care systems. At the same time, informal carers' access to services in their own right has become more difficult. These policy settings have created new tensions for the way in which carers combine their paid work and unpaid care and undermine the economic security of informal carers.

Consumer-directed care and the marginalisation of carers' (work) needs

The dominant trend in disability and aged care policy in Australia towards consumer-directed care has created a strong tension in the policy landscape in supporting work–care reconciliation among informal carers. The introduction of new consumer-directed-style care systems in disability and home-based aged care has had some positive outcomes for people with disability and older people who have received an individual plan or package of services (Mavromaras et al. 2018). However, the reconfiguration of the policy landscape has marginalised the needs of carers, especially their work needs. For carers of the majority of people with disability or chronic illness *without* an NDIS package, and for carers of older people who do not use aged care services, there is no access to carer services through these systems. Carers who do provide care for a person using these systems can only access supports or services for their own needs in very limited circumstances, such as to support them in their care activities. At the same time, for many carers, while the new disability and home-based aged care systems have provided packages of support to their loved ones, it has not necessarily reduced the amount of time they spend on their care responsibilities. For many carers, while the nature of the care they provide may have changed, such as providing less physical care, the time they spend caring has stayed the same or *increased* because they need to spend a large amount of time navigating, communicating with and monitoring services (Hamilton 2018).

A central part of this tension concerns access to respite, perhaps the most important service enabling carers to participate in paid work. A strong assumption underpinning the consumer-directed model of care provision is that services that better meet the needs of the consumer (i.e., the person with disability or the older person) will have a secondary effect of supporting the carer (Hamilton et al. 2016). That is, providing services to the consumer will result in a "respite effect" for the carer, providing them with a break while the care recipient engages in activities focused on their own needs. In the case of the NDIS, for example, policymakers argued that providing better formal support services to people with disability would "free up" their family carers for participation in paid work (i.e., Kelly 2017; Reference Group on Welfare Reform 2014: 31).

However, the new disability and aged care service infrastructures have in many instances made it *more* rather than less difficult for carers to participate in paid work. The new Carer Gateway does provide services directly to carers based on their specific needs, and some services provided through the Gateway – such as career advice, financial support for training and access to planned respite – may support some carers to participate in paid work. However, access to planned respite that enables carers to be absent from the care recipient for the periods of time necessary to participate in paid work (Pickard et al. 2018) remains extremely low, undermining (mostly) women carers' opportunities to combine work with care and achieve economic security.

Working longer, caring longer: work–care reconciliation among mature-age workers

A second tension emerges from the dual imperatives of increasing the involvement of informal carers in the care of relatives and extending working lives in the context of an ageing population and increases in life expectancy (Productivity Commission 2011: 132). Governments are strongly promoting the extension of working lives and have introduced a number of measures to incentivise delayed retirement, such as raising the pension eligibility age (Hamilton & Suthersan 2020). Yet, while older Australians are remaining in the paid workforce for longer, there is also an increased reliance on them as carers – and carers are more likely than non-carers to retire early (Welsh et al. 2018).

Rates of informal care of a person with disability or an older person generally increase with age, with almost one in five people aged 55 to 64 providing care to a person with disability or an older person (Australian

Bureau of Statistics 2018). Women are more likely to be carers than men (Australian Bureau of Statistics 2018). Carers, particularly primary carers, are less likely to be in the labour force and less likely to be employed than non-carers (Australian Bureau of Statistics 2018).

Maintaining employment can be important for mature-age workers' incomes and retirement security, quality of life and self-esteem as well as having broader benefits for gender equality (Eurofound 2015; Australian Human Rights Commission 2013a). Workers aged 55 and over have a strong preference for working part-time, with care for relatives cited as one of the main reasons (Cassidy & Parsons 2017). However, international evidence suggests carers are more likely to leave employment than reduce their work hours when they take on caring roles (Colombo et al. 2011).

While there is increasing focus on work–care reconciliation policies that support parents of young children, work–care reconciliation in later life remains on the fringe of policy attention and effort. Support for mature-age working carers requires not only appropriate long-term care services for people with disability and older people (and children, recognising the role played by grandparents in child care), but also specific measures to support mature-age carers' rights to economic and social participation, including flexible support and accountability for carer wellbeing in care systems (Carers Australia 2020); workplace policies that support retention and flexibility, including transition to retirement; support for carers re-entering the labour force; and income support and retirement incomes.

Interrogating the notion of the care-friendly workplace

Limitations in the Australian regulatory framework for worker-carers reflect the way in which provisions favour full-time and longer term continuous employment, excluding many worker-carers, particularly women, who are more likely to hold non-standard jobs (Chapman 2018). There is also a lack of adequate and effective enforcement provisions. Chapman (2018) argues that such shortcomings underpin the failed Australian attempt to substantially dislodge the male breadwinner–female homemaker framework. This example of institutionalised gender inequality significantly affects worker-carers whose carer responsibilities, which may change over time in both intensity and frequency, are poorly recognised in employment regulation and policy.

Flexibility that enables worker-carers to exert some control over their working time or place provides a critical foundation for their own job quality and for their roles as informal carers (Pocock & Charlesworth 2017). However, both anti-discrimination and employment regulation provides only for individual accommodations rather than the setting of standards envisaged under ILO Convention No. 156 on Workers with Family Responsibilities. Indeed, such accommodations have for the most part worked to either exclude or "adapt" worker-carers to the demands of substantially unchanged workplaces and institutions (Charlesworth & Macdonald 2017). Moreover, the non-standard employment of many worker-carers means that they often lack the basic working-time security to meet their care obligations. This pressure is illustrated vividly in a recent study of the clash of fluctuating working-time schedules with care responsibilities in retail (Cortis et al. 2021). Such pressure compromises the capacity of worker-carers to achieve income and working-time security and to meet both predicable and unpredictable demands for care.

The existing system of workplace leaves is also inadequate for meeting the needs of informal carers. As discussed above, current leave provisions in the National Employment Standards are not accessible by all workers and those who do have access to personal/carers leave only have access to 10 days leave per year, reduced on a pro-rata basis for part-time workers. As working carers are more likely to work part-time (Australian Bureau of Statistics 2018), they have access to fewer days per year. Many carers, most of whom are women, thus have inadequate leave to meet their care responsibilities, particularly those experiencing periods of intensive need by a family member or caring for a family member at the end of life (Hamilton & Broom 2021). In addition, because personal/carers leave comprises *both* sick leave and leave to care for others, many carers are forced to use all this leave to provide care and consequently do not have any leave left to meet their own health needs (Australian Human Rights Commission 2013b; see also Chapter 2). This is all the more problematic as carers are more likely than non-carers to experience poor health and wellbeing. An

Australian study found that carers had poorer self-rated health, socio-economic status and quality of life as well as lower life satisfaction than non-carers (O'Loughlin et al. 2017). Inadequate access to leave for care and ill health can drive carers out of the labour market.

The de-valuing of paid care and its implications for the work–life balance of informal carers

An important aspect of formal care systems, with implications for informal carers, is the extent to which paid care work is valued. Undervaluing of paid care work creates gaps and deficiencies in formal care provision that are left to be filled by informal carers.

Long-standing gendered inequalities in Australia's treatment of the feminised care workforce have seen care workers' pay and conditions fall behind other occupations. A significant but partial remedy for gendered undervaluation of pay occurred in 2012 when unions won the Social and Community Services Equal Remuneration Case, with the support of a federal Labor government that committed to providing funding for pay increases (Cortis & Meagher 2012). However, this remedy did not apply to the many frontline care workers who are classified as home care workers in the industrial award. As a result of this, in 2021, home care workers' pay rates are up to 25 per cent less than other social and community services workers and are barely more than the minimum wage (Charlesworth 2021: 6–7).

Undervaluing does not only manifest in low pay for paid care workers, it also plays out in lack of recognition of skills, inadequate time for workers to provide care and poor working-time standards that allow fragmented and unpredictable work schedules (Macdonald et al. 2018). Thus, undervaluation influences unpaid or *informal* care loads as informal carers must compensate for the inadequacies of paid care provision, including that their care work time can mirror the fragmented and unpredictable schedules of paid care workers.

Undervaluation of care work is evident in funding systems as well as in wage-setting and other aspects of industrial regulation. Within the individualised disability support and aged care schemes, funding rarely accounts for the relational aspects of care and the articulation work required to manage tasks and social processes involved in the work.

Cost containment imperatives drive minimisation of allocated time for care, including through care being defined as a narrow set of tasks that receive funding allocations for very short blocks of time. These also contribute to extra pressure on carers to smooth gaps in formal service systems. The undervaluation of paid care work contributes to the wider lack of recognition of the importance of all care (formal and informal) to families, communities and economies.

6.5 Avenues for change

As the population ages and the need for aged and disability care increases, the strains on the system become more apparent. Many carers are already at breaking point. Improving the circumstances of carers requires a recalibration of Australia's policy infrastructure, including the strengthening of formal aged and disability care services and better support for carers inside and outside of workplaces.

Currently, disability and aged care systems are designed in ways that place undue pressure on family carers to fill gaps and navigate complex and inadequate service landscapes, limiting opportunities for carers to engage in paid employment. Paid disability and aged care work must be better recognised and resourced as an essential and productive activity to improve the working conditions of paid care workers, and the quality, access and affordability of care services for people with disability and older people. The fragmented care markets generated by the current funding structures not only reduce the conditions of paid care workers and the quality and accessibility of formal care, they create additional pressure on informal carers. Funding structures that provide more resources to aged and disability care and enable less fragmented forms of care would reduce pressure on informal carers and increase opportunities for combining unpaid care with work.

Carers must also be integrated into long-term care systems, including adequate recognition and consultation, recognition that consumer and carer needs may be connected in complex ways, and acknowledgement of carers' needs and rights to support for social and economic participation. This would challenge the focus on the individual inherent in consumer-directed care models, and assert the importance of relationality, connectedness and community. A move away from the focus on the consumer to focus on the care dyad would also place a greater focus on the undue pressure placed on carers by the current formal service system.

In addition to the formal disability and aged care systems, an improved and integrated policy architecture for carers must focus more heavily on support for informal carers to maintain work and build careers. Currently, support for carers to participate in paid work is limited and patchy. This requires better resourcing of the Carer Gateway (and/or other systems) and the provision of adequate replacement care, in contrast to the continued focus of respite care on "short breaks" that are inadequate for supporting carers to participate in paid work in an ongoing way. It also requires integrated support across the aged, disability and carer service systems and a recognition of the importance of palliative care to all systems.

Greater support is also required to improve the employment participation and economic security of carers inside and outside of paid work. If worker-carers are to enjoy a better quality of working life over the life course, a right to give and receive care needs to be enshrined in employment regulation and institutional arrangements at the macro-social and economic levels (Busby 2018; Pocock & Charlesworth 2017). A right to care would require a strong scaffolding of paid leaves and *non-negotiable* working-time rights which are accessible by all worker-carers whatever their employment status (Pocock & Charlesworth 2017: 40). Improvements to carer leave provisions were recommended by the Royal Commission into Aged Care Quality and Safety (2018–21) and were the subject of a Productivity Commission inquiry in 2022, but the focus has been on unpaid leave. Reform of paid carers leave is a much more important component, which needs to be designed on the assumption that all workers engage in unpaid care for others, with women no longer expected to take on the economic burden of unpaid care (Fudge 2014: 20). As Rubery (2015) argues, policies that normalise the combining of work and care would further encourage gender equality in the sharing of these essential roles.

References

Aged Care Financing Authority (2021). *Ninth Report on the Funding and Financing of the Aged Care Industry*. Canberra: Commonwealth of Australia.

Australian Bureau of Statistics (2018). *Disability, Ageing and Carers, Australia: Summary of Findings, 2018*. https://bit.ly/3rL1qFG.

Australian Human Rights Commission (2013a). *Investing in Care: Recognising and Valuing Those Who Care, Volume 1 Research Report*. Sydney: Australian Human Rights Commission. https://bit.ly/3RyX5zx.

Australian Human Rights Commission (2013b). *Investing in Care: Recognising and Valuing Those Who Care, Volume 2 Technical Papers*. Sydney: Australian Human Rights Commission. https://bit.ly/3RyX5zx.

Australian Institute of Health and Welfare (2020). Aged care data snapshot. https://bit.ly/3t4WBrn.

Brennan, D., Charlesworth, S., Adamson, E. and Cortis, N. (2017). Out of kilter: changing care, migration and employment regimes in Australia. In S. Michel and I. Peng, eds. *Gender, Migration, and the Work of Care*, 143–65. Cham, Switzerland: Palgrave Macmillan.

Broady, T., and Weber, N. (2021). Carers missing out: a scoping study following the introduction of the National Disability Insurance Scheme, Prepared for the NSW Carers Advisory Council, NSW Department of Communities and Justice.

Busby, N. (2018). The evolution of gender equality and related employment policies: the case of work–family reconciliation. *International Journal of Discrimination and the Law* 18(2–3): 104–23.

Campanella, N. and Edmonds, C. (2021). COVID-19 vaccine rollout for people living with disability "seriously deficient", royal commission report finds. *ABC News*, 27 September. https://bit.ly/3RvNIAy.

Campbell, I. and Charlesworth, S. (2020). The National Employment Standards: an assessment. *Australian Journal of Labour Law* 33(1): 1–16.

Carer Respite Alliance (2021). *Repositioning Respite in Consumer Directed Service Systems*. Sydney: Carers NSW.

Carers Australia (2020). *Pre-Budget Submission, August 2020*. https://bit.ly/3TgrEuW.

Cassidy, N. and Parsons, S. (2017). The Rising Share of Part-Time Employment. *Bulletin*, September Quarter 2017. Reserve Bank of Australia. https://bit.ly/3RxJd8w.

Chapman, A. (2018). Work-and-care initiatives: flaws in the Australian regulatory framework. *Journal of Law and Equality* 14(1): 115–43.

Charlesworth, S. (2021). Supplementary statement of Sara Catherine Mary Charlesworth, Fair Work Commission Matter No: AM2021/65, Application to vary the Social, Community, Home Care and Disability Services Industry Award. https://bit.ly/46NZTNh.

Charlesworth, S. (2011). Law's response to the reconciliation of work and care: the Australian case. In C.G. James and N. Busby, eds. *Families, Care-giving and Paid Work: Challenging Labour Law in the 21st Century*, 86–103. Cheltenham: Edward Elgar Publishing.

Charlesworth, S. and Elder, A. (2012). Convention no. 156 and recommendation no. 165: Australia. In A. Cruz, ed. *Good Practices and Challenges on the Maternity Protection Convention, 2000 (No. 183) and the Workers with Family Responsibilities Convention, 1981 (No. 156): A Comparative Study*, 79–102. Geneva: International Labour Organization.

Charlesworth, S. and Macdonald, F. (2017). Employment regulation and worker-carers: reproducing gender inequality in the domestic and market spheres? In D Peetz, and G Murray, eds. *Women, Labor Segmentation and Regulation*, 79–96. New York: Palgrave Macmillan.

Clun, R. (2022). "Inadequate" support for aged care as COVID crisis continues. *Sydney Morning Herald*, 7 February. https://bit.ly/46CXFAQ.

Colombo, F., Llena-Nozal, A., Mercier, J. and Tjadens, F. (2011). *Help Wanted? Providing and Paying for Long-Term Care*. Paris: OECD.

Constantin, A., Hamilton, M., Zettna, N., Baird, M., Dinale, D., Gulesserian, L., Williams, A. (2022). Looking beyond hours of care: the effects of care strain on work withdrawal among Australian workers. *International Journal of Care and Caring* 6(3): 318–34.

Cooper, R. and Baird, M. (2015). Bringing the "right to request" flexible working arrangements to life: from policies to practices. *Employee Relations: The International Journal* 37(5): 568–81.

Cortis, N., Blaxland, M. and Charlesworth, S. (2021). *Challenges of Work, Family and Care for Australia's Retail, Online Retail, Warehousing and Fast-food Workers*. Sydney: Social Policy Research Centre, UNSW Sydney.

Cortis, N. and Meagher, G. (2012). Recognition at last: care work and the equal remuneration case. *Journal of Industrial Relations* 54(3): 377–85. https://doi.org/10.1177/0022185612442278.

Da Roit, B. and Moreno-Fuentes, F.J. (2019). Cash for care and care employment: (missing) debates and realities. *Social Policy and Administration* 53(4): 596–611.

Deloitte Access Economics (2020). *The Value of Informal Care in 2020*. Carers Australia. https://bit.ly/4a8mhE9.

Department of Social Services (2021). *NDIS National Workforce Plan: 2021–2025*. Canberra: Department of Social Services. https://bit.ly/46O0vm3.

Eagar, K., Westera, A., Snoek, M., Kobel, C., Loggie, C. and Gordon, R. (2019). *How Australian Residential Aged Care Staffing Levels Compare with International and National Benchmarks*. Wollongong: Centre for Health Service Development, Australian Health Services Research Institute, University of Wollongong.

Eggers, T., Grages, C., Pfau-Effinger, B. and Och, R. (2020). Re-conceptualising the relationship between de-familialisation and familialisation and the implications for gender equality – the case of long-term care policies for older people. *Ageing and Society* 40(4): 869–95.

Eurofound (2015). *Working and Caring: Reconciliation Measures in Times of Demographic Change*. Luxembourg: Publications Office of the European Union.

Fine, M. and Davidson, B. (2018). The marketization of care: global challenges and national responses in Australia. *Current Sociology* 66(4): 503–16, https://doi.org/10.1177/0011392118765281.

Fudge, J. (2014). Feminist reflections on the scope of labour law: domestic work, social reproduction, and jurisdiction. *Feminist Legal Studies* 22(1): 1–23.

Hamilton, M. (2018). The NDIS hasn't made much difference to carers' opportunities for paid work *The Conversation*, 2 October. https://bit.ly/46KV1ZX.

Hamilton, M. and Broom, A. (2021). "They died surrounded by family and friends (who could get leave from work if they needed)". *Croakey*, 22 March. https://bit.ly/46FUtEv.

Hamilton, M., Giuntoli, G., Johnson, K., Kayess, R. and Fisher, K.R. (2016). *Transitioning Australian Respite* (SPRC Report 04/2016). Sydney: Social Policy Research Centre, UNSW Australia.

Hamilton, M. and Suthersan, B. (2021). Gendered moral rationalities in later life: older women balancing work and care of grandchildren in Australia. *Ageing and Society* 41(7): 1651–72.

Henriques-Gomes, L. (2020). Australians with disabilities missing out on essential services as Covid-19 crisis escalates. *Guardian*, 17 March. https://bit.ly/45qp2Nv.

Jefferson, T. (2009). Women and retirement pensions: a research review. *Feminist Economics* 15(4): 115–45.

Kelly, C. (2017). Interview on *ABC Lateline*, February. https://bit.ly/4822d4g.

Macdonald, F. (2021). *Individualising Risk: Paid Care Work in the New Gig Economy*. Singapore: Palgrave Macmillan.

Macdonald, F., Bentham, E. and Malone, J. (2018). Wage theft, underpayment and unpaid work in marketised social care. *The Economic and Labour Relations Review* 29(1): 80–96. https://doi.org/10.1177/1035304618758252.

Malbon, E., Carey, G. and Meltzer, A. (2019). Personalisation schemes in social care: are they growing social and health inequalities? *BMC Public Health* 19(1): 805. https://doi.org/10.1186/s12889-019-7168-4.

Mavromaras, K., Moskos, M., Mahuteau, S. and Isherwood, L. (2018). *Evaluation of the NDIS Final Report*. Adelaide: National Institute of Labour Studies, Flinders University.

Meagher, G. (2021). A genealogy of aged care. *Arena Quarterly* 6. https://arena.org.au/a-genealogy-of-aged-care/.

Meagher, G., Cortis, N. Charlesworth, S. and Taylor, W. (2019). *Meeting the Social and Emotional Support Needs of Older People Using Aged Care Services*. Sydney: Macquarie University, UNSW Sydney and RMIT University.

National Disability Insurance Agency (2019). *Access to the NDIS – The Disability Requirements*. National Disability Insurance Agency. https://bit.ly/46NRfhZ.

National Disability Insurance Agency (n.d.). *Including Specific Types of Supports in Plans Operational Guideline – Sustaining Informal Supports*. National Disability Insurance Agency. https://bit.ly/46FCJsP.

Needham, C. (2011). *Personalising Public Services: Understanding the Personalisation Narrative*. Bristol, UK: Policy Press.

Oliver, S., Gosden-Kaye, E., Winkler, D. and Douglas, J. (2020). The outcomes of individualized housing for people with disability and complex needs: a scoping review. *Disability and Rehabilitation*. https://bit.ly/3uS7o8P.

O'Loughlin, K., Loh, V. and Kendig, H. (2017). Carer characteristics and health, wellbeing and employment outcomes of older Australian baby boomers. *Journal of Cross-Cultural Gerontology* 32(3): 339–56.

Perlow, L. and Kelly, E. (2014). Toward a model of work redesign for better work and better life. *Work and Occupations* 41(1): 111–34.

Pickard, L., Brimblecombe, N., King, D. and Knapp, M. (2018). "Replacement care" for working carers? A longitudinal study in England, 2013–15. *Social Policy and Administration* 52: 690–709.

Pocock, B. and Charlesworth, S. (2017). Multilevel work–family interventions: creating good-quality employment over the life course. *Work and Occupations* 44(1): 23–46.

Productivity Commission (2011). *Disability Care and Support*, Report No. 54. Canberra: Australian Government.

Reference Group on Welfare Reform (2014). *A New System for Better Employment and Social Outcomes*. Interim Report of the Reference Group on Welfare

Reform to the Minister for Social Services, Commonwealth of Australia. https://bit.ly/4a7W4FJ.

Royal Commission into Aged Care Quality and Safety (2021). *Final Report: Care Dignity and Respect – Volume 2: The Current System*. Canberra: Commonwealth of Australia.

Rubery, J. (2015). Regulating for gender equality: a policy framework to support the universal caregiver vision. *Social Politics: International Studies in Gender, State and Soci*ety 22(4): 513–38.

Sixsmith, A. and Sixsmith, J. (2008). Ageing in place in the United Kingdom. *Ageing International* 32: 219–35.

Skatssoon, J. (2019). Carers sidelined by Home Care Package program. *Ageing Agenda*, 2 May. https://bit.ly/3Gx8gSH.

Skinner, N. and Pocock, B. (2014). *The Persistent Challenge: Living, Working and Caring in Australia in 2014. The Australian Work and Life Index*. Adelaide: Centre for Work+ Life, University of South Australia.

Temple, J. and Dow, B. (2018). The unmet support needs of carers of older Australians: prevalence and mental health. *International Psychogeriatrics* 30(12): 1849–60. https://doi.org/10.1017/S104161021800042X.

Tune, D. (2019). *Review of the National Disability Insurance Scheme Act 2013*. Canberra: Department of Social Services. https://bit.ly/46DYR75.

University of Canberra and NATSEM (2021). *Caring for Others and Yourself: The 2021 Carer Wellbeing Survey*. Canberra: Carers Australia. https://bit.ly/41kcdE8.

Warr, D., Dickinson, H., Olney, S. et al. (2017). *Choice, Control and the NDIS: Service Users' Perspectives on Having Choice and Control in the New National Disability Insurance Scheme*. Melbourne: University of Melbourne.

Welsh, J., Strazdins, L., Charlesworth, S., Kulik, C.T. and D'Este, C. (2018). Losing the workers who need employment the most: how health and job quality affect involuntary retirement. *Labour and Industry: A Journal of the Social and Economic Relations of Work* 28(4): 261–78.

Workplace Gender Equality Agency (2019). *Australia's Gender Equality Scorecard. Key Findings from the Workplace Gender Equality Agency's 2018–19 Reporting Data*. https://bit.ly/3Rc9s34.

7

Tax and welfare policy: Removing embedded gender inequalities in work and care

Miranda Stewart

7.1 Introduction

Australia's tax and welfare policy framework is often referred to as the "tax and transfer system", which refers to the raising of revenue by the Australian government through taxes and the redistribution of funds through social security (or welfare) payments called "transfers". Australia's tax and transfer system affects most people over the course of their lives by levying tax on income from work and saving; providing income support to relieve poverty or where work is not possible or available; delivering support for care of children; and supporting people in their old age.

This chapter outlines the current dynamics of Australia's tax and transfer system and demonstrates the impact these policies have on the work and care outcomes of women, and their families. It shows that Australia's tax and transfer policies are not gender-neutral. Instead, despite incremental reforms, tax and transfer policies for work and care are outdated, discouraging women's paid market work and reinforcing gendered structures of responsibility for care of children by women in the home. This produces lifelong unequal outcomes for women and men.

The chapter begins with an overview of Australia's tax and transfer policies for work and care, focusing on the structure of income tax rates, the Medicare levy, family assistance payments and the child care subsidy. Discussion shows how the combination of these policies produces high effective tax rates on women's labour income and creates a strong disincentive for women to increase their participation in paid work. These policy settings continue to favour either a "breadwinner–homemaker" where women are not in paid work and have full responsibility for care of children and the home, or the "1.5 earner" family model in which women are secondary earners who retain primary responsibility for the care of children at home. The chapter then explores the tensions embedded in tax and transfer policies around work and care, showing how current policies skew the economic playing field in favour of men over the life course. This undermines both gender equality and Australia's capacity to achieve shared and sustainable economic prosperity as we enter an era of population ageing and declining fertility. The final section presents avenues for change in tax and transfer policy so the cost of care is shared between men and women and across society.

7.2 Australia's tax and transfer system for work and care

The Commonwealth government is responsible for Australia's tax and transfer systems directly relevant to work and care. These include income tax, the Medicare levy, social security, child care and family assistance payments (Apps 2017; Australian Treasury 2008). In the 2021–22 year, income tax raised 70 per cent of Commonwealth revenue (Australian Treasury 2023a: 185, Table 5.7). In the income tax itself, more than 60 per cent is raised from personal income tax on individuals, especially labour income, while the remainder is raised from company tax. Taxes raised go into consolidated general revenue reported in the annual Commonwealth budget, which is then appropriated by legislation of the Australian Parliament to deliver public goods, services and social security payments.

Australia's social security system delivers cash transfers, or welfare payments, to individuals and families based on need, measured by income and asset tests and other eligibility criteria. Social security is the largest single Commonwealth function and in 2021–22 it absorbed

$226 billion, more than one third of its expenditure (Australian Treasury 2023b: 177, Table 6.3). Importantly, in Australia, social security payments are funded out of general revenues, which is unlike the system in many other OECD countries, where social security is financed by a specific social insurance fund comprising separate tax contributions from workers and employers.

State, territory and local governments also have a variety of taxes such as stamp duties and land tax, but about half of their budgets comprise grants appropriated by the Australian Parliament out of Commonwealth taxes. The states and territories share responsibility with the Commonwealth government for other policies and expenditure affecting families with children, including health, schooling and funding for preschool (see Chapter 4).

This chapter focuses on Australia's tax and transfer policies that are directly relevant to work and care. This includes two taxes and three social security payments. Parental leave pay, another social security payment, was discussed in Chapter 3. The following policies are discussed:

1. Income tax levied on an individual at progressive rates, under the *Income Tax Assessment Act 1936* (Cth), *Income Tax Assessment Act 1997* (Cth) and the *Income Tax Rates Act 1986* (Cth) (collectively, the "income tax");
2. Medicare levy of 2 per cent on individuals under the *Medicare Levy Act 1986* (Cth);
3. Family assistance payments provided to eligible families with children, income-tested on the joint income of a couple, under the *A New Tax System (Family Assistance) Act 1999* (Cth) (the "*Family Assistance Act*"). This includes two payments that have different eligibility criteria, Family Tax Benefit A ("FTB A") and Family Tax Benefit B ("FTB B");
4. Child Care Subsidy ("CCS"), a payment for eligible families, income-tested on the joint income of a couple and other criteria, and paid directly to child care centres under the *Family Assistance Act*;
5. Parenting payment for low-income parents with a child under the age of eight (if a single parent) or six (if a partnered parent), under the *Social Security Act 1991* (Cth).

Income tax and the Medicare levy

The income tax applies to an individual based on their taxable income, calculated on earned (and other) income, minus allowable deductions such as work-related expenses. In general, policies that provide support for families are not delivered through the income tax law. An individual taxpayer who supports a relative with a disability, or a carer of such a relative, may be eligible for a dependent tax offset but this does not apply for care of minor children. Historical provisions such as dependent spouse or child rebates have been repealed over time (Stewart 1999). The cost of child care is not an allowable tax deduction because, like expenses of commuting, food and the home, child care fees are treated as private costs that are not incurred in the course of earning income. There has been an ongoing debate about the deductibility of child care costs, discussed later in this chapter.

The income tax rate structure applicable to individuals is progressive, meaning that both the marginal tax rate and the average tax rate increase as an individual's taxable income increases. The *marginal* tax rate is the tax rate that would apply to the individual's next dollar of taxable income, while the *average* tax rate is the total tax paid by the individual as a percentage of their total taxable income. Australia's progressive rate structure has a tax-free threshold below which no income tax is paid, currently $18,200. Above this threshold, there are increasing marginal tax rates rising to a top marginal rate of 45 per cent for taxable income over $180,000 (see Table 7.1).

The progressive tax rate structure is complicated by the addition of tax offsets for low-income earners that taper as income increases. A tax offset reduces the amount of tax owed by the taxpayer, in contrast to a deduction which reduces income subject to tax. Tapering refers to a process of reducing the amount received in social security benefits as income increases. Individuals with taxable income below $66,667 are eligible for the Low Income Tax Offset (LITO), which tapers to zero, depending on income. In addition to income tax, there is the Medicare levy of 2 per cent, which is levied on the taxable income of individuals and is, in effect, a surcharge on the income tax. A reduced Medicare levy applies for very low-income families; this benefit is also tapered as income rises.

Table 7.1 Tax rates for individual residents of Australia, 2021–22 compared to 2024–25

Taxable income	Tax rates 2021–22	Taxable income	Tax rates 2024–25
0 – $18,200	Nil (tax-free threshold)	0 – $18,200	Nil
$18,201 – $45,000	19 per cent tax rate	$18,201 – $45,000	19 per cent tax rate
$45,001 – $120,000	32.5 per cent tax rate	$45,001 – $200,000	30 per cent tax rate
$120,001 – $180,000	37 per cent tax rate		
$180,001 and over	45 per cent tax rate	$200,001 and over	45 per cent tax rate

Australia's income tax rate structure has been subject to significant change over the last decade, almost always reducing the income tax rates. The most recent change was the "three-stage" tax cuts legislated by the Morrison government in 2018 (Griffiths & Wood 2020; Stewart 2018; *Treasury Laws Amendment (Personal Income Tax Plan) Act 2018*). The first two stages of these tax cuts raised the income threshold for the 32.5 per cent tax rate and enacted a temporary Low and Middle Income Tax Offset (LMITO), which expired in the 2021–22 tax year. Stage 3 of the tax cut plan was legislated to take effect for the 2024–25 income year. Unless the Albanese government introduces legislation to amend it, stage 3 will remove the 37 per cent tax rate, lower the 32.5 per cent rate to 30 per cent, increase the threshold for that rate, and increase the threshold for the top rate of 45 per cent. The rate structure for the 2021–22 year compared to the legislated rate structure proposed for the 2024–25 year is presented in Table 7.1.

Transfers: Family assistance

The main family assistance payments provided by the Commonwealth government are Family Tax Benefit A (FTB A) and Family Tax Benefit B (FTB B). These benefits are paid fortnightly as cash transfers to eligible families to assist with the cost of raising children. Both FTB A and FTB

B are means-tested based on a joint (couple) unit, which combines the adjusted taxable income of both members of a couple, or the individual income of a single parent. Eligibility for these payments also depends on the number and age of dependent children and the work and residence status of parents.[1] Table 7.2 summarises the key dimensions of FTB A and FTB B.

Parenting payment is an additional social security payment that mainly applies to support sole (unpartnered) parents with young children. Once children are age eight years or over, sole parents must rely on the general JobSeeker (unemployment) payment, plus FTB A and FTB B, for income support.

---

1   See summary of terms for these payments here: Services Australia,
      Parenting Payment, https://www.servicesaustralia.gov.au/parenting-payment;
      Family Tax Benefit, https://www.servicesaustralia.gov.au/family-tax-benefit;
      Child Care Subsidy, https://www.servicesaustralia.gov.au/child-care-subsidy.

Table 7.2 Summary of family assistance payments

Payment	Eligibility	Payments	Taper rate	Who benefits
FTB A	Paid to families supporting children aged 0–12 or dependent students aged 16–19. Income test based on the joint income of both members of a couple, or of a sole parent.	Maximum rate applies up to $58,108 joint income of a couple, partnered family, or single-parent income: • $197.96/fortnight, $5,197/year (0–12) • $257.46/fortnight, $6,694/year (12–15; dependent students 16–19) • Base rate above $58,108 is $1,653/year.	Taper rates and thresholds depend on the number and age of children: • Taper at 20 per cent (payment is reduced by 20 cents for each dollar of income) for family income up to $103,368 • Taper at 30 per cent for family income from $103,369, until reduced to nil.	In June 2022, 1.4 million families received FTB A, split evenly between partnered and unpartnered families.
FTB B	Paid to primary carer in partnered families supporting children up to age 13, and single-parent families up to age 19.	Maximum rate: • $168/fortnight, $4,375/year (0–5) • $117/fortnight, $3,054/year (5–13, partnered	Income test for couples: • Primary earner: taper at 20 per cent up to a maximum of $104,432/year	In June 2022, around 1.1 million families received FTB B, 38 per cent partnered and 62 per cent unpartnered.

151

Payment	Eligibility	Payments	Taper rate	Who benefits
	Income test based on the joint income of both members of a couple. Not payable while receiving parental leave pay.	family; up to 19, single parent)	• Secondary earner, eligible up to $6,059/ year, then taper at 20 per cent to $29,985/ year (0–5) or $23,360 (5–13), when eligibility ceases.	A family loses entitlement once secondary earner returns to part-time work.
CCS	Paid for families with a child aged 13 or younger who is not attending secondary school, using an approved child care service and other criteria. Benefit varies depending on eligibility and requires primary carer to meet minimum work or study obligations, with some exceptions.	CCS covers a proportion of child care fees up to an hourly rate cap based on the type of care. Hourly cap of $12.74 per hour for eligible centre-based long day care. Usually, parents must pay for 10 hours per day even if they do not use the full day of care.	Covers up to 85 per cent of the hourly fee up to the cap, for joint couple income up to $70,015. Means-tested on joint couple income, tapered at 1 per cent for every $3,000 of joint income over $70,015. Covers between 85 per cent and 50 per cent of the hourly fee up to the cap for joint income up to $177,466.	Estimated to be delivered to about 1.1 million families in 2021. CCS is more widely available to middle- and upper-income families than FTB A and FTB B, as indicated by the higher joint income thresholds. However, the level of CCS per child is significantly reduced as couple income rises to average full-time wages for each member of the couple.

Payment	Eligibility	Payments	Taper rate	Who benefits
	Where there is more than one child aged 5 or younger in child care, a 30 per cent higher subsidy applies for the second or further children, up to a cap of 95 per cent of the cost of care for that child.	Hourly cap for family day care is $11.80. Hourly cap for outside school hours care is $11.15.	Covers 50 per cent or less of the hourly fee up to the cap for joint income above $177,466, reducing to nil at joint income of $356,756.	

Unpartnered parents receive reduced family assistance if child support payments are owed from parents who are not the primary carers.[2] In this way, the child support scheme reintroduces a form of "couple" or joint unit for some unpartnered parents. Other social security payments may also be important for low-income families, especially JobSeeker for sole parents with children aged eight and over and rent assistance for low-income families who do not own a home and are not eligible for public housing.

Transfers: Child Care Subsidy (CCS)

The Child Care Subsidy (CCS) is the main way that the Commonwealth government assists families with the cost of child care. The CCS is available for children from infancy to age five, and for primary school students using out of school hours (before or after school) care (see Chapter 4 of this volume). Eligibility for CCS is determined by applying a means test to the joint income of both members of a couple, for a partnered family, or the individual income of a single parent, and it is then paid directly to child care centres. The CCS tapers as the joint income of a couple increases, over a base threshold, until eligibility ceases.

The CCS aims to make child care more affordable and, in so doing, support gender equality and women's economic security. The main way it is intended to do this is by promoting women's paid workforce participation, and this aim is reinforced by minimum hours, work and study obligations for CCS eligibility. The CCS delivers a substantial subsidy to many families, with the maximum benefit targeted to low-income families. Despite this, it only partly achieves its aims of gender equality and promoting women's workforce participation. This is because income testing for CCS, based on the parameters summarised in Table 7.2, has the effect of reducing the amount of subsidy when the secondary earner (usually the mother) seeks to increase hours of paid market work; that is, when the need and cost of child care is greatest. Consequently, women with young children perceive the cost of child care as a penalty for increasing their hours of work and therefore decide to not participate further in the labour

---

2   Services Australia, *Child Support Assessment*, https://bit.ly/489ZRQT.

market. This reinforces a traditional male breadwinner–female homemaker model. Changes to the scheme introduced in March 2022 mean the CCS now applies to a higher proportion of middle-income families than previously, but many families continue to face a substantial net child care cost (see Chapter 4).

A policy design that produces high effective tax rates, discouraging women's paid work

Most families with children are affected by the mix of tax and transfer policies described above, with secondary earners (mostly mothers) often facing very high effective marginal tax rates. High marginal tax rates are the outcome of the "quasi-joint" tax and transfer unit that is produced by the interaction of income tax and family benefit policies where income tax rules are applied to individual earners in the family and the calculation of family payments and CCS is applied to the joint (couple) unit. The "effective tax rate" is the term used to describe the total of the applicable income tax rate and taper rates that reduce the CCS and family assistance as joint income increases.

The secondary earner in a family is usually the mother, so the high effective tax rates produced by the tax and transfer system disproportionately affect women, compounding gender inequality in the labour market. This effect can be illustrated by an example of a couple family on average wages, with two children under the age of five, based on policies and wage rates applicable as at March 2022. Assume that the primary earner in the family (usually male) earns the average male wage of $95,500 (full-time). He pays income tax on this wage at a *marginal* tax rate of 34.5 per cent, being the 32.5 per cent marginal tax rate as indicated in Table 7.1, plus the Medicare levy of 2 per cent. The primary earner faces an *average* tax rate of just under 25 per cent, calculated as the total tax paid by him as a share of his taxable income and including the Medicare levy. Assume that the secondary earner in the family (usually female) could earn a wage of about $83,000 if she worked full-time. We are interested in the effective tax rate faced by the secondary earner as she increases her days of paid work from one day up to five days a week.

As the secondary earner starts to earn income from working one, then two, days per week, her wages will exceed the tax-free threshold of $18,200, and she will begin to pay income tax at the 19 per cent tax rate, plus the Medicare levy. The family is eligible for the CCS to assist in covering the cost of child care for the days that she is at work. The CCS covers child care fees at a maximum of 85 per cent of a benchmark fee, tapering to below 50 per cent of the fee as the secondary earner's income increases with more days of work a week (see Table 7.2). While the family benefits from the CCS, they lose family assistance as the secondary earner's income rises. When the secondary earner was not doing any paid work, the family's eligibility for FTB A and FTB B was tested solely on the primary earner's income. As a result of the secondary earner's entry into paid work, each day's earnings are added on top of the primary earner's income and the family loses FTB A and FTB B at 20 or 30 cents in the dollar until the payment is reduced to nil.

Figure 7.1 presents the effective tax rate faced by the secondary earner for each additional day of work a week (from one day to five days). Figure 7.1 shows that the effective tax rate on wages earned by the secondary earner working one day a week is 44 per cent. This is a consequence of the family losing FTB A (dark grey) and FTB B (light grey) and paying child care fees net of the CCS (chequered). The effective tax rate on wages earned by the secondary earner up to three days a week is similar, but is the result of different elements of the tax and transfer policy mix. At three days a week, the family is no longer eligible for FTB A or FTB B, because these payments have tapered to zero under the joint income test, while the level of CCS is tapered below 50 per cent of the child care fee for the two children. While a tax rate of 44 per cent is already high for the secondary earner who, at three days work a week, is earning about the minimum wage, a dramatically higher tax rate is produced at days four and five of work. The net cost of child care (after the reduced CCS is applied), income tax and the Medicare levy, pushes the effective tax rate on the secondary earner close to 70 per cent as she increases her work hours from part-time to full-time work. This means that the family takes home just over 30 per cent of the secondary earner's wage for the fourth and fifth days of work, net of taxes and transfers.

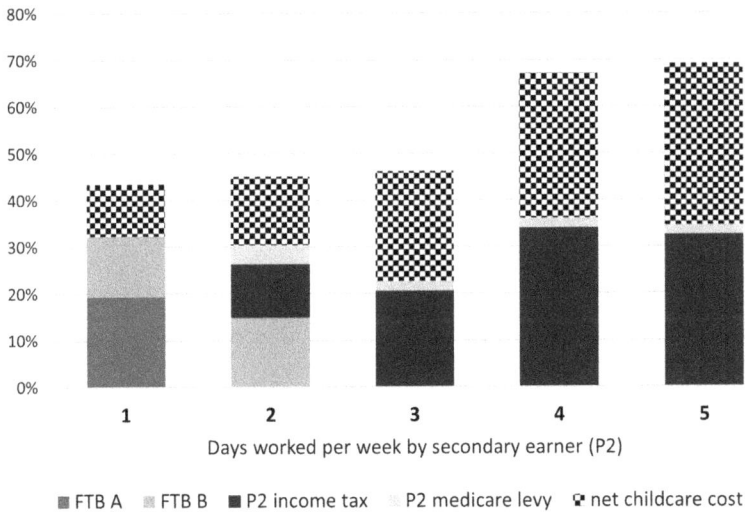

80%
70%
60%
50%
40%
30%
20%
10%
0%

1   2   3   4   5

Days worked per week by secondary earner (P2)

■ FTB A   ▨ FTB B   ■ P2 income tax   P2 medicare levy   ✿ net childcare cost

Figure 7.1 Effective tax rate on seconday earner, by day worked, average wage couple. Created by David Plunkett and Miranda Stewart.

Notes: Thresholds and payments at March 2022. The daily marginal tax rate is measured on increment of one day's income and net child care cost. P1 (primary earner) income is $95,500 per year; P2 (secondary earner) income is $16,600 per day worked per year, up to full-time average female earnings of $83,000. Two children, aged 2 and 3. Child care is estimated at $10.50 per hour per child, and long day care is modelled at 10 hours per day. The CCS covers up to 85 per cent of the first child, and up to 95 per cent for the second child, up to the income thresholds.

The secondary earner's wage is excessively taxed because of these policy effects. The effective daily tax rate of nearly 70 per cent on the secondary earner's wage for days four and five of work is twice the marginal tax rate faced by the primary earner on his wage, which is 34.5 per cent including the Medicare levy. The secondary earner's effective *average* tax rate if she were to work full-time (her total combined taxes and loss of benefits as a share of income) exceeds 50 per cent, twice the average tax rate faced by the primary earner of just under 25 per cent. Indeed, the effective tax rates faced by the secondary earner at an average female wage are higher than the tax rates faced by the highest income earners in Australia. Because men generally earn more than women, this inequity will be exacerbated by the Stage 3 tax cuts due to take effect in 2024–25, which will consequently have significantly gender-unequal effects (Grudnoff 2022).

7.3 Policy tensions and debates

The policy design of Australia's tax and transfer system for work and care is complex and reveals tensions between goals of budgetary restraint, equity, efficiency, and gender equality in work and care. Current policies embed contradictory goals of encouraging women's workforce participation as a key plank of delivering gender equality while retaining a systemic expectation that women will continue to have primary responsibility for the care of children.

Targeted versus universal support for care

Australia has the most tightly targeted social security system in the Organisation for Economic Co-operation and Development (OECD) (Stewart & Whiteford 2018), due to strict eligibility requirements, means-testing and steep taper rates for most Australian welfare payments. Australia is also relatively parsimonious in overall expenditure on social security, spending relatively less as a percentage of GDP on welfare payments compared to other OECD countries (OECD 2019).

Family assistance and the CCS are targeted to low- and moderate-income families by testing on the joint income of a couple. Targeting income support to the poorest helps to ensure that the least well off are protected. For many low-income families, FTB A and FTB B provide substantial income support and help to prevent child poverty, although failure to index the payments to inflation and increases to the tapering rates make these payments less effective than when originally designed. The tight means-testing of family assistance and other payments reduces the cost to the federal budget and enables higher payments to be targeted to low-income families.

Assistance for families with children is estimated to cost the Commonwealth budget $39.6 billion in 2022–23 and is forecast to increase to $52.2 billion in 2026–27 (Australian Treasury 2023b, 19, Table 6.9). This is about half the cost of federal assistance for aged care and significantly less than the cost of assistance for care of people with disabilities (see Chapter 6 in this volume). Targeting family assistance payments and CCS by tapering payments based on joint income is efficient in the fiscal sense of keeping budgetary costs down, but it can only achieve this because it shifts the cost of care onto women inside the family. This means current tax and transfer policy settings constrain women's participation in employment, imposing significant costs to economic productivity and prosperity as well as to the wellbeing of individual women and their families. The current system therefore imposes a specific economic cost on dual-earner couples who seek a more egalitarian sharing of work and care and undermines the progressivity of the tax and transfer system.

Economic security for women over the life course

Tax and transfer policies that discourage women's paid work do not only affect women caring for young children. The policy interactions explained in this chapter have significant life course effects that shape women's economic security in older age (Kalb 2017). Women are more likely to make the constrained choice to stay home rather than participate in paid work, and this is the major cause of the gender gap in retirement savings through Australia's superannuation system. Many women leave the labour market entirely for long periods, or their paid work hours are reduced when there are preschool (and school) age children in the family and never recover to a full-time level (Bahar et al. 2022). This causes a substantial loss in total income for women, as well as a loss of taxes to the government (Apps 2022). While out of the labour market, the professional skills and education of women may dwindle in value and be lost to the economy.

Australia's Superannuation Guarantee requires employers to contribute to a superannuation fund for individual workers based on their wage income. Women's pattern of lower workforce participation than men due to care of children or others (see Chapters 4 and 6 in this volume), combined with their over-representation in part-time, casual and low-paid feminised sectors, leads to a significant gender gap in retirement savings as a result of lower lifetime wages, a gap which widens through prime child-rearing ages from 30 to 50 years. In 2022, the gap between median superannuation balances of men and women at age 60 was 23.4 per cent (Clare 2022). Women who do not have sufficient superannuation savings rely on the publicly funded age pension, which itself is means-tested and tapers according to an income and assets test.

Current superannuation tax policy extends a large subsidy to high-income earners, who can save substantial amounts which are taxed at lower rates and draw down large superannuation pensions in a tax-free manner in retirement (for a detailed discussion, see Ingles & Stewart 2017). Reducing the gap in lifetime earnings between women and men, mainly by supporting women back into paid work, would assist in reducing gender inequality in superannuation savings and economic security over the life course. Other policies include extending superannuation to paid parental leave (see Chapter 3 in this volume). It is important to remember that women who have spent a lifetime caring for children and others will rely on the age pension in retirement, so ensuring adequacy in the age pension is also important for gender equality.

Tax and transfer policies in an era of population ageing and declining fertility

Australia's tax and transfer policy settings also have implications for long-term equity and prosperity in the context of Australia's ageing population and declining fertility. Australia's total fertility rate (the proportion of children per woman) declined from 3.3 in 1965 to 1.69 in 2021–22, well below the usual replacement rate of 2.1, and consistent with worldwide trends (Australian Treasury 2023c, Chart 2.8; and see McDonald & Hosseini-Chavoshi 2022; Ritchie et al. 2022; and Chapter 2 in this volume). Lower fertility, combined with Australia's increasingly long-lived and ageing population, increases the total dependency ratio, which is the ratio of the dependent population (assumed to be those under the age of 15 and those over the age of 65) to the working-age population. Since 2010, Australia's total dependency ratio has increased as we have fewer children and live longer (Stewart 2021). This poses a challenge for economic wellbeing, as today's children will form the labour force and will contribute future income tax revenue out of which aged pensions and public services are provided.

The COVID-19 pandemic has reminded us of the essential value of care work – both paid and unpaid – and highlighted that without care the economy crumbles (Work + Family Policy Roundtable 2020). The Australian time-use survey indicates that the share of time on domestic work and care activities by women is 61.9 per cent, compared to 41.1 per cent by men (Risse 2023; ABS 2021). In today's demographic context, governments need to make policy changes to support national wellbeing in the longer term. The cost of care for children has become increasingly visible but policymakers are still paying inadequate attention to the role of tax and transfer policy for work and care in determining the conditions for family formation.

7.4 Avenues for change

Addressing gender inequality in the tax and transfer system should aim to support a more equitable sharing of the cost and time of care between men and women. As Nussbaum (2002: 134) has argued, sharing the cost of care should be at the centre of policymaking, as a good society must arrange to provide care for those in a condition of extreme dependency, without exploiting women and depriving them of the capability to participate in paid work. In contrast to the viewpoint that the state is subsidising carers through the CCS and family payments, it is the unpaid carers – of children and others – who are subsidising the state and the economy by ensuring that society can continue to thrive (Fineman 2005). Taking the long-term view, demographers suggest that ensuring a stable and age-balanced population in Australia, even with significant ongoing immigration, requires "substantial social and economic transformations that ...

involve reducing the opportunity costs of having children, family-friendly working conditions, employment security for young people, housing costs, and gender equity" (McDonald & Hosseini-Chavoshi 2022: 15).

In this context, we should seek to enact policies that will equitably increase women's participation in paid work – which will deliver greater economic security for women while also enhancing economic growth, increasing disposable income of families with children – and grow tax revenues in the medium and long term (Dixon 2020; OECD 2017). Crucially, these policies must support families raising children by redistributing public resources for care across the life course and across the population, rather than continuing to privatise the cost of children, which places the burden of care on women (see Chapter 4 in this volume).

The problem of high effective tax rates for secondary earners in Australia's tax and transfer system is not caused by the income tax itself. The two main policies identified in this chapter that cause high effective tax rates and require attention if we are to achieve gender equality in work and care are the net cost of child care (despite increasing subsidies) and the design of family assistance payments.

The cost of child care

One often-proposed policy is to permit tax deductibility of child care fees. As discussed above, child care fees are not deductible because they are considered a private expense insufficiently linked to earning income. Some have disputed this approach, arguing child care is essential for women to participate in paid work (e.g., Thiagarajah & Selvarajah 2021). The Commonwealth Parliament could legislate a deduction for all or part of child care fees, effectively delivering a subsidy for this cost through the income tax system. However, there are several reasons why this would not be a sufficient or equitable solution to the problem. First, a tax deduction is regressive. A deduction of $100 is worth $47 to a high-income taxpayer on the top marginal tax rate of 45 per cent, plus the 2 per cent Medicare levy, but only $19 to a low-income taxpayer on the 19 per cent tax rate, while it is worth nil to someone earning below $30,000 a year due to the tax-free threshold and LITO (see Table 7.1 above). Consequently, a tax deduction for child care costs would not assist a low-earning secondary earner who pays relatively little income tax, while a tax deduction allowed against joint income or the primary earner's income would benefit high-income families much more than low-income families. Replacing the CCS with a tax deduction would make all but the top 20 per cent of income-earning households worse off than current policy (Wood et al. 2020: 54, 86). Finally, a tax deduction is a fiscally costly strategy that would require regulation and capping to prevent excessive deduction by high-income earners using luxury child care services.

An alternative could be a child care tax credit, or offset, which would reduce the tax owed rather than reduce the taxable income of the secondary earner. This would be more equitable than a deduction. A child care tax credit could be made "refundable", which is essentially the same as delivering a cash transfer or subsidy. However, because the income tax is assessed on an annual basis, a child care tax credit would be paid only once a year on filing a tax return. In contrast, the CCS is payable fortnightly. A child care tax credit would likely be means-tested to contain the cost, as is the CCS. This would, itself, generate high effective tax rates on the secondary earner's income, although these may be less pronounced if the credit is tested on the secondary earner's individual income rather than on joint couple income.

It is important to recalibrate current tax and transfer policy design because gender inequality related to child care affects all families and cuts across class. The last five years have seen a series of incremental expansions of the CCS, while still failing to deliver a suitable policy to support workforce participation. The Morrison government's expansion of the CCS in the lead-up to the May 2022 federal election responded to political demands following a period of free child care during the COVID-19 crisis (see Chapter 4 in this volume). This change was part of a series of incremental expansions of the CCS, which have had the effect of sharing the cost of care of children across the taxpaying population of Australia. The Albanese Labor government, elected in May 2022, expanded CCS further to cover 95 per cent of the child care hourly fee (retaining the fee cap as is current policy).[3] This was estimated to cost an additional $4.5 billion over four years.[4] In the October 2022–23 Women's Budget Statement it was observed that "affordable and accessible early childhood education and care is critical social infrastructure that supports gender equality" (Australian Treasury 2022: 1). Despite this expansion and improvement, the Albanese government has retained the core design features of the CCS, including means-testing on joint income. Further expansion of the CCS is recommended (see KPMG 2019).

If the government's concern for short-term fiscal cost implies that income testing must be maintained, there are two ways forward. One would be to test the payment based on the secondary earner's income, rather than on the joint income of the couple or the primary earner's income, thus reducing the effective tax rate on mothers. The second and preferred approach is the universal public provision of child care. The apparent inequality of higher income families receiving universal benefits can be addressed by ensuring that higher incomes are taxed through progressive income tax rates. We can contrast the debates about targeting and constraining the fiscal cost of the CCS to Australia's commitment over more than a century to universal free school education. Universal early childhood education and care, largely delivered as a public service, would eliminate half of the high effective tax rates faced by women as secondary earners. It would free up sole parents who are expected to work while also managing significant care responsibilities, and who are often poor. It would also relieve some in older generations – mostly women – from the informal burden of grandchild care, enabling them to continue paid work and helping to ensure their own economic independence and security. In the long term, investment in a universal publicly funded early childhood education and care system, as advocated by most experts (see Chapter 4 in this volume), would deliver significant returns in economic growth and tax revenues.

---

3   See *Family Assistance Legislation Amendment (Cheaper Child Care) Bill 2022* (Cth), https://bit.ly/48qiwIH.

4   Department of Education, *Federal Budget commits $4.5 billion for more affordable child care*, https://bit.ly/471YZgy.

Family assistance payments

Children are priceless, of course, to their parents, but they are also valuable for society and the economy, as explained above. As such, it is appropriate for society to assist families with the cost of raising children. Australia's increasingly inadequate and tightly targeted family assistance delivered in FTB A and FTB B is failing to achieve this goal for many families. Increasingly tight income-testing on combined family income means just over half of all children in Australia receive these payments, in contrast to full coverage until the 1980s (Stewart et al. 2023; Stewart & Whiteford 2018). Current policy design embeds a full-time breadwinner–part-time worker/homemaker model of the family and contributes to the high effective tax rates faced by secondary earners seeking to increase their hours of work (Hodgeson 2008).

Australia historically had a system of universal child allowances. The first income-testing of these allowances was in 1987 by the Hawke Labor government, which aimed to deliver benefits to the poorest families and manage the fiscal cost by reducing benefits across the board. Under subsequent governments, the increase in taper rates and a failure to index thresholds and quantum of payments reduced this support.

One potential reform is to abolish FTB B and remodel FTB A into a universal, or close to universal, child payment. One way to constrain fiscal cost could be to make this universal payment taxable based on the individual income of the secondary earner. This approach has the advantage of applying a progressive income tax rate structure, smoothing the tax rates faced by the secondary earner while ensuring that higher income families would benefit less, and lower income families more. It would be important to ensure that other payments, such as Parenting Payment, are sufficient to protect children in low-income families from poverty, especially in sole-parent families (the majority of whom are women). Many of the same policy prescriptions apply for sole parents as for secondary earners in couple families. There are good reasons to encourage paid market work by sole parents, including to increase the income and long-term economic security of those families. The economic wellbeing of sole parents can be protected by retaining and strengthening their connection to the labour market, education and career development. However, it is also important to acknowledge the particular work and care challenges faced by single parents, who may also be escaping family violence. Therefore, single parents who bear an extra burden of care should be supported to a greater extent in their parenting role beyond when their child turns eight.

7.5 Conclusion: Financing universal benefits with a progressive income tax

Universal child care and family assistance can be financed by strengthening and maintaining the progressive income tax and broadening its base. Potential tax reforms to the base could include taxing accumulated superannuation savings and other capital income more highly – the subject of recent debate. A progressive and adequate tax rate structure for earned income is also crucial. Specifically, the abolition, whether in whole or part, of the Stage 3 tax cuts in 2024–25 would finance a significant proportion of the cost in each year. The cost of the Stage 3 tax cuts to the government budget is estimated to cost from $17 billion to $36 billion a year, a total of $243 billion over the 10 years from its commencement (Parliamentary Budget Office 2022). Some of the revenue from the Stage 3 tax cuts could be redirected to fund universal child care. The redirection of public revenue would deliver a tax cut to those who need it most, and who are most likely to respond to a reduction in the work disincentive; that is, secondary earners in families with children – women.

Australia, like many other developed economies, is over-invested in private care for children and under-invested in public care for both children and the elderly (Gal et al. 2018; and see Chapters 4 and 6 in this volume). The uneven distribution of public and private investment in the care of the young and elderly in Australia shows that the traditional "breadwinner–homemaker" care bargain is both unsuitable and unfair in an era of declining fertility. Current tax and transfer policy settings overburden families and lead to the over-specialisation of women in the care of children in the home, and the under-utilisation of women's labour in the market (e.g., Apps 2017; Apps & Rees 2010). Women bear a disproportionate share of the financial and time cost of care and do not fully benefit from the economic independence, reward or security that come with having a full-time, well-paid job over the life course.

When designing solutions for these challenges, we need to be explicit about the costs and trade-offs in our tax and transfer policies. Instead of continuing to embed gender inequality, the Australian government has an opportunity to reform tax and transfer policy to share the cost of care and remove barriers to economic security and wellbeing for women. A more universal approach to the delivery of child care and family assistance offers many benefits from the perspective of children, parents, the economy and gender equality.

References

Apps, P. (2022). Optimal tax design: choice of tax base and rate structure. *Australian Tax Review* 51(2): 103–17.

Apps, P. (2017). Gender equity in the tax-transfer system for fiscal sustainability. In Miranda Stewart, ed. *Tax, Social Policy and Gender: Rethinking Equality and Efficiency.* Canberra: ANU Press.

Apps, P. and Rees, R. (2010). Australian family tax reform and the targeting fallacy. *Australian Economic Review* 43(2): 153–75.

Australian Bureau of Statistics (2022). *How Australians Use Their Time.* 2020–21 Time Use survey, released 7 October 2022. https://bit.ly/3ThYLhU.

Australian Treasury (2023a). *Budget 2023–24, Budget Paper 1, Statement 5: Revenue,* https://budget.gov.au/content/bp1/index.htm

Australian Treasury (2023b). *Budget 2023–24, Budget Paper 1, Statement 6: Expenses and Net Capital Investment,* https://bit.ly/47NXoMl.

Australian Treasury (2022). *Budget October 2022-23, Women's Budget Statement.* https://bit.ly/3NeHYZi.

Australian Treasury (2023). *2023 Intergenerational Report.* https://bit.ly/3Ryqg5x.

Australian Treasury (2008). *Architecture of Australia's Tax and Transfer System,* Report of the Review of Australia's Future Tax System (August 2008). https://bit.ly/3TfAhWr.

Bahar, E., Bradshaw, N., Deutscher, N., Montaigne, M. (2022). Children and the gender earnings gap. Treasury Round Up, October. https://bit.ly/4abSnPb.

Clare, R. (2022). *Developments in Account Balances: Superannuation Account Balances for Various Demographic Groups.* March. ASFA Report. https://bit.ly/47YoUGK.

Dixon, J. (2020). *A Comparison of the Economic Impacts of Income Tax Cuts and Childcare Spending.* 15 October. Report for the Australia Institute. https://bit.ly/48Nvt0a.

Fineman, M. (2005). Cracking the foundational myths: independence, autonomy, and self-sufficiency. In M. Fineman and T. Dougherty, eds. *Feminism Confronts Homo Economicus: Gender, Law, and Society,* 179–92. Ithaca, NY: Cornell University Press.

Gál, R.I., Vanhuysse, P. and Vargha, L. (2018). Pro-elderly welfare states within child-oriented societies. *Journal of European Public Policy* 25(6): 944–58.

Griffiths, K. and Wood, D. (2020). *Explainer: The Argument over Personal Income Tax Cuts.* Grattan Institute. https://bit.ly/3uLz3br.

Grudnoff, M. (2022). *Rich Man's World: Gender Distribution of the Stage 3 Tax Cuts.* Australia Institute, February. https://bit.ly/3Gx8BEX.

Hodgeson, H. (2008). More than just DNA – Tax, welfare and the family. An examination of the concept of family in the tax transfer system, with particular reference to family benefits. *Australian Journal of Social Issues* 43(4): 601–614.

Ingles, D. and Stewart, M. (2017). Reforming Australia's superannuation tax system and the age pension to improve work and savings incentives. *Asia and the Pacific Policy Studies.* https://doi.org/10.1002/app5.184.

Kalb, G. (2017). Taxes, transfers, family policies and paid work over the female life cycle. In Miranda Stewart, ed. *Tax, Social Policy and Gender: Rethinking Equality and Efficiency,* 133–160. Canberra: ANU Press.

KPMG (2019). *Unleashing our Potential: The case for further investment in the child care subsidy.* KPMG Australia; Chief Executive Women.

McDonald, P. and Hosseini-Chavoshi, M. (2022). What level of migration is required to achieve zero population growth in the shortest possible time? Asian examples. *Frontiers in Human Dynamics* 4, Article 762199: 1–16.

Nussbaum, M. (2002). Capabilities and social justice. *International Studies Review* 4: 123–35.

OECD (2019). *Society at a Glance 2019: OECD Social Indicators.* Paris: OECD Publishing. https://doi.org/10.1787/soc_glance-2019-en.

OECD (2017). *The Pursuit of Gender Equality: An Uphill Battle.* Paris: OECD Publishing. http://doi.org/10.1787/9789264281318-en.

Parliamentary Budget Office (2022). Stage 3 tax cuts distributional analysis. Request for budget analysis, Mr Adam Bandt MP, Australian Greens, released 7 July 2022.

Risse, L. (2023). *By how much is "women's work" undervalued in the economy? And why does it matter?* Paper presented at Australian Conference of Economists. Brisbane (9–12 July 2023).

Ritchie, H., Mathieu, E., Rodes-Guirao, L. and Gerber, M. (2022). Five key findings from the 2022 UN Population Prospects. Our World in Data, 11 July. https://ourworldindata.org/world-population-update-2022.

Stewart, M. (2021). *Tax and the Fertility Freefall: Children, Care and the Intergenerational Report.* Melbourne School of Government Policy Brief No. 13, 14 July.

Stewart, M. (2018). Personal income tax cuts and the new Child Care Subsidy: do they address high effective marginal tax rates on women's work? Tax and Policy Institute, ANU, TTPI Policy Brief 1/2018, August. https://bit.ly/3uNjPmr.

Stewart, M. (1999). Domesticating tax reform: the family in Australian tax and transfer law. *Sydney Law Review* 21(3): 453–86.

Stewart, M., Porter, E., Bowman, D., Millane, E. (2023) *Growing Pains: Family Tax Benefit issues and options for reform.* Brotherhood of St Laurence (forthcoming).

Stewart, M. and Whiteford, P. (2018). Balancing equity and efficiency in the tax and transfer system. In Breunig, Robert and Fabian, Mark eds. *Hybrid Public Policy Innovations: Contemporary Policy Beyond Ideology*, 204–31. London: Routledge.

Thiagarajah, L. and Selvarajah, A.D. (2021). COVID-10 and childcare expense deductions: revisiting the decision in Lodge. *Australian Tax Review* 50: 51–80.

Wood, D., Griffiths, K. and Emslie, O. (2020) *Cheaper childcare: A practical plan to boost female workforce participation.* Melbourne: Grattan Institute.

Work + Family Policy Roundtable (2020). *Work and Care in a Gender Inclusive Recovery: A Bold Policy Agenda for a New Social Contract.* https://bit.ly/3RziatE.

Contributors

Editors

Professor Marian Baird AO (University of Sydney)
Marian is an international leader in research on industrial relations, women, work and care across the life course. She is Australia's leading scholar on parental leave, working with governments, unions and employers for several decades on supporting women at this critical stage of their reproductive lives. Marian has a strong history of policy and research impact in Australia and globally and is a Coordinator of both the International Network of Leave Policies and Research and the International Labour and Employment Relations Association Gender and Employment Study Group. In March 2023 Marian was appointed as a member of the Fair Work Commission Expert Panel and will sit on the Annual Wage Review Panel.

Professor Elizabeth Hill (University of Sydney)
Elizabeth is a leading researcher on the future of women, work and care in Australia and the Asian region and has a strong history of research leadership in this field. She is founder and co-convenor of the Australian Work and Family Policy Roundtable and Deputy Director of the Gender Equality in Working Life (GEWL) Research Initiative at the University of Sydney, a multidisciplinary research initiative identifying

drivers and obstacles to gender equality at key transition points in working life and practical workplace interventions. In 2018 she co-founded the landmark Body@Work project developing new research evidence on workplace policy supports for reproductive wellbeing and gender equality. Elizabeth has extensive research experience on women's working lives, including as Chief Investigator of the Australian Research Council (ARC) Gender and the Future of Work Project, which includes the development of a new empirical database and academic analysis of women's career aspirations and the future of women's work in Australia, Japan and the United Kingdom.

Ms Sydney Colussi (University of Sydney)
Sydney is a PhD candidate at the University of Sydney and early career scholar in the fields of socio-legal and policy studies at the forefront of research in the area of gender, work and reproductive health. She is co-convenor of The Body@Work Project, an interdisciplinary research group focused on work, reproductive wellbeing and gender equality and member of the Women, Work and Policy Research Group and Work + Family Policy Roundtable. She holds a Juris Doctor from the University of Sydney Law School and BA Political, Economic and Social Sciences (Hons I) from the University of Sydney Faculty of Arts and Social Sciences. Sydney is a regular commentator on public and workplace policies for reproductive wellbeing.

Contributing Authors

Dr Elizabeth Adamson (University of New South Wales)
Elizabeth is a Research Fellow at the Social Policy Research Centre (SPRC). She has expertise in comparative care and family policy including: early childhood education and care (ECEC), the social and political economy of formal and informal care, and gender, migration and care. She is interested in how policy systems and programs interact and impact the lives and decisions of families and different demographic groups.

Professor Emerita Deborah Brennan AM (University of New South Wales)
Deborah Brennan is one of Australia's leading researchers in comparative welfare, family policy and gender and politics. Deborah has held visiting positions at the London School of Economics, Oxford University, Trinity College Dublin and the University of Melbourne. She is the author of *The Politics of Australian Child Care* (Cambridge University Press, 1998) and co-editor with Louise Chappell of *"No Fit Place for Women"*. *Women in New South Wales Politics, 1856–2006* (UNSW Press, 2006) as well as numerous scholarly articles in the areas of gender, politics and family policy. In February 2023, Deborah was appointed as an Associate Commissioner with the Productivity Commission to work on the Early Childhood Education and Care inquiry.

Professor Emerita Sara Charlesworth (RMIT University)
Sara is a socio-legal scholar whose research focuses on gender (in)equality in employment at the labour market, industry and organisational levels. She has held two Australian Research Council fellowships, including a Future Fellowship (2013–2018), and held ARC projects on sexual harassment, gender equality and decent work, frontline care work, migrant care workers, and quality part-time work. Sara is currently co-convenor of the Work + Family Policy Roundtable, a network of Australian gender, work and care scholars, and is on the editorial board of the *Journal of Industrial Relations*.

Professor Rae Cooper AO (University of Sydney)
Professor Rae Cooper, AO is Professor of Gender, Work and Employment Relations. She is based in the Discipline of Work and Organisational Studies (WOS) at the University of Sydney Business School. Rae is a leading researcher in the world of work and has a particular interest in women's career navigation, the gendered experience of professions and occupations and the gendered nature of employment policy and regulation. She is an Australian Research Council Future Fellow (2022–2025), Director of the Gender Equality in Working Life (GEWL) Research Initiative, and President Elect of the Executive Committee of the International Labor and Employment Relations Association. She is a member of the national Women's Economic Equality Taskforce.

Associate Professor Myra Hamilton (University of Sydney)
Associate Professor Myra Hamilton is a Principal Research Fellow at the ARC Centre of Excellence in Population Ageing Research, in the Discipline of Work and Organisational Studies at the University of Sydney Business School. She is a sociologist and social policy researcher whose research focuses on gender, ageing, work and care. She is Reviews Editor of the *International Journal of Care and Caring* and sits on the NSW Carers Advisory Council and the Board of COTANSW. Prior to the University of Sydney, Myra worked for 11 years at the Social Policy Research Centre at the University of New South Wales.

Dr Frances Flanagan (University of Technology Sydney)
Frances Flanagan is a Lecturer in Law at the University of Technology Sydney. With an interdisciplinary background in law and history, Frances' research focuses on the intersection of industrial relations and climate change, digital technologies and neoliberal institutional orders. She was the guest co-editor of a 2023 special issue of the *Journal of Industrial Relations* entitled 'Climate Change and Industrial Relations', as well as the author of articles published in journals that include *New Technology Work and Employment, Labour History, Journal of Industrial Relations, Thesis Eleven, History Australia, Public History Review* and *The Economic and Labour Relations Review.*

Dr Meraiah Foley (University of Sydney)
Dr Meraiah Foley is a Senior Lecturer in the Discipline of Work and Organisational Studies at the University of Sydney Business School and a member of the Gender Equality in Working Life Research Initiative. Her research focuses on gender equality at work, the gendered impacts of workplace technological change, and women's experiences working in male-dominated occupations and industries. Dr Foley is a Chief Investigator on two Australian Research Council (ARC) grants and a University of Sydney Business School grant focused on increasing women's participation in cybersecurity careers.

Dr Fiona Macdonald (Centre for Future Work)
Fiona is Policy Director with the Centre for Future Work, a research centre within the independent public policy think tank, The Australia Institute. Fiona is an adjunct Principal Research Fellow at RMIT University. Fiona has held academic positions in employment and

industrial relations at RMIT and the University of South Australia as well as research, policy and leadership roles in social and community services and vocational education and training sectors. She has written extensively on women, work and industrial relations, including on social care employment, insecure work, wage theft, gig work and contracting, equal pay, collective bargaining and low-paid workers. Fiona is a member of the Australian Work and Family Policy Roundtable research network of academics with expertise on work, care and family policy.

Professor Miranda Stewart (University of Melbourne)
Miranda Stewart is a Professor at Melbourne Law School, The University of Melbourne, where she is Director of Tax Studies and the Melbourne Centre for Commercial Law. Miranda is an Honorary Professor at the Crawford School of Public Policy, The Australian National University, with the Tax and Transfer Policy Institute. Miranda was the inaugural Director of the Institute from 2014 to 2017. Miranda engages in research, policy advice and teaching across a wide range of topics on taxation law and policy, budgeting and public finance. Recent authored or edited books include *Tax and Government in the 21st Century* (2022, Cambridge University Press) and *Tax, Social Policy and Gender* (2017, ANU Press).

Professor Emerita Gillian Whitehouse (University of Queensland)
Gillian Whitehouse is Professor Emerita in the School of Political Science and International Studies, The University of Queensland. Her research focuses on gender pay equality and the gendered impacts of parental leave and related employment entitlements, both in Australia and cross-nationally. She has undertaken national and international consultancies in these areas and published widely on gender equality themes.

Index